WHITE MUSLIM

WHITE MUSLIM
FROM LA TO NEW YORK...TO JIHAD?

BY BRENDAN BERNHARD

MELVILLE HOUSE PUBLISHING
HOBOKEN, NEW JERSEY

PORTIONS OF THIS BOOK HAVE APPEARED, IN SOMEWHAT DIFFERENT
FORM, IN *LA WEEKLY.*

BOOK DESIGN BY DAVID KONOPKA

MELVILLE HOUSE PUBLISHING
300 OBSERVER HIGHWAY
THIRD FLOOR
HOBOKEN, NEW JERSEY 07030

FIRST PRINTING
ISBN 10: 0976658356
ISBN 13: 9780976658351

A CATALOG RECORD FOR THIS BOOK IS
AVAILABLE FROM THE LIBRARY OF CONGRESS.

PRINTED IN CANADA

CONTENTS

FOR IRENE

THE "OTHER"
SEPTEMBER 11 EFFECT

In a stunningly perverse way, the attacks of September 11, 2001, constituted the greatest religious infomercial the world has ever seen. If all publicity is good publicity, then 9/11 was an act of publicity on the level of an act of God. Islam was not simply in the news, it *was* the news, to the exclusion of almost everything else. And if the news seemed uniformly bad, if a small number of Muslims were being abused and attacked, there were nonetheless benefits for the many Muslims committed to *da'wa*, namely, the propagation of their faith. Americans, in particular, became interested in Islam as never before, and there is believed to have been a sharp increase in the number of people converting to the religion worldwide.

No less an authority than Osama bin Laden took note of the post-9/11 conversion phenomenon. In Holland, he told his al-Qaeda lieutenants on a video later released by the Pentagon, "the number of people who accepted Islam during the days that followed the operations was more than the people who accepted Islam in the last 11 years. I heard someone on Islamic radio who owns a school in America say: 'We don't have time to keep up with the demands of those who are asking about Islamic books to learn about Islam.' This event made people think [about true Islam], which benefited Islam greatly."[1]

September 11 wasn't, in other words, entirely bad news for the Muslim community in the West, which, until then, had been one of the least prized and politically potent pieces in American multiculturalism's "gorgeous mosaic." The attack on Pearl Harbor in World War II led to the internment of

Japanese Americans, but the destruction of the

World Trade Center led Americans down a very different path. As the Palestinian-American commentator Anayat Durrani wrote at the time, "America opened the book on Islam [and] the Islamic faith became almost as much a story as the tragedy itself." Though he was preparing to invade Afghanistan and eventually Iraq, President Bush went out of his way to term Islam "a religion of peace" and dissuade Americans from taking their anger out on Muslim immigrants. On September 14, a somber interfaith prayer service was held at Washington National Cathedral, with several former American presidents in attendance and a prominent Muslim imam, Muzammil Siddiqi, taking part. On September 23, an even bigger memorial service took place at Yankee Stadium. It included recitations from the Koran and a sermon by the imam of Harlem's Masjid Malcolm Shabazz Mosque. Beamed via television into millions of homes, this sudden elevation of Islam in American life, with the haunting sound of the Islamic call to prayer rising from the most fabled sports arena in the country, was moving to some, disturbing to others. It was, after all, in Islam's name—"true" Islam, according to bin Laden—that America had just been set upon.

It was also reported that the number of people converting to Islam doubled, tripled, even quadrupled in the days and weeks following the attacks. In Holland, it was rumored that 30,000 had done so. Two months later, Nihad Awad, the executive director of the influential Council on American-Islamic Relations (CAIR), put the figure of post-9/11 American conversions at 34,000. Meanwhile, in the London-based Arab daily, *Al-Hayat*, CAIR's Alaa Bayumi wrote about the tragedy's aftermath in prose that, far from communicating shame or guilt or horror, radiated pride and confidence and hope:

"Non-Muslim Americans are now interested in getting to know Islam. There are a number of signs...: Libraries have run out of books on Islam and the Middle East...English translations of the Koran head the American best-seller list...The Americans are showing increasing willingness to convert to Islam since September 11...Thousands of non-Muslim Americans have responded to invitations to visit mosques, resembling the waves of the sea [crashing on the shore] one after another...All this is happening in a political atmosphere that, at least verbally, encourages non-Muslim Americans' openness towards Muslims in America and in the Islamic world, as the American president has said many times in his speeches...."

On September 22, 2001, Dr. Walid A. Fitaihi, then an instructor of medicine at Harvard Medical School (he has since moved to Saudi Arabia, trailed by charges of anti-semitism and political extremism), published a letter in the Egyptian weekly *Al-Ahram Al-Arabi*, describing the aftermath of 9/11 in Boston and elsewhere from a Muslim perspective. Initially, Fitaihi wrote, it seemed that "proselytizing in the name of Allah had been set back 50 years in the U.S. and in the entire world." But within four days of the attacks, there were signs of hope, of what Hisham Aidi of Columbia University's Middle East Institute has termed "the other September 11 effect." Namely, an unexpected interest and increase in conversions by Americans to the religion in whose name they had just been assaulted.

"On Saturday, September 15," Fitaihi wrote, "I went with my wife and children to the biggest church in Boston, [Trinity Church] in Copley Square, by official invitation of the Islamic Society of Boston, to represent Islam by special invitation of the senators of Boston. Present were the mayor of Boston, his wife, and the heads of the universities. There were more than 1,000 people there, with media coverage by one of Boston's main television stations. We were received like ambassadors. I sat with my wife and children in the front row, next to the mayor's wife. In his sermon, the priest defended Islam as a monotheistic religion, telling the audience that I represented the Islamic Society of Boston....

"After the sermon was over, he stood at my side as I read an official statement issued by the leading Muslim clerics condemning the incident [*i.e.,* the attacks]. The statement explained Islam's stance and principles, and its sublime precepts. Afterwards, I read Koran verses translated into

English... These were moments that I will never forget, because the entire church burst into tears upon hearing the passages of the words of Allah!

"Emotion swept over us. One said to me: 'I do not understand the Arabic language, but there is no doubt that the things you said are the words of Allah.' As she left the church weeping, a woman put a piece of paper in my hand; on the paper was written: 'Forgive us for our past and for our present. Keep proselytizing to us.' Another man stood at the entrance of the church, his eyes teary, and said, 'You are just like us; no, you are better than us.'"

Fitaihi obviously found American self-abasement to his liking. In the manner of an excited missionary reporting back to camp, he went on to describe other meetings held over the following week by the Islamic society of Boston and the Islamic Center in Cambridge, Massachusetts, where he was repeatedly stunned by the good will and interest in Islam expressed by non-Muslim American attendees, which at one event included 300 students as well as Harvard faculty and the American ambassador to Vienna.

"Proselytizing in the name of Allah has not been undermined, and has not been set back 50 years, as we thought in the first days after September 11," he concluded. "On the contrary, the 11 days that have passed are like 11 years in the history of proselytizing in the name of Allah. I write to you today with the absolute confidence that over the next few years, Islam will spread in America and in the entire world, Allah willing, much more quickly than it has spread in the past, because the entire world is asking, 'What is Islam!'"[2]

What indeed? And, to ask a politically incorrect question, what does it want? No one knows for sure how many people in America and elsewhere have converted to Islam, and probably less is known about white and Latino converts than any other group. But it is clear that one thing Islam wants is to establish itself in America on an equal footing with the two other "Abrahamic" religions, Judaism and Christianity, and then comprehensively surpass them. That such an idea can even be entertained is largely the result of the immense sums of Saudi Arabian money which have poured into the creation of mosques, Islamic cultural centers, charities, foundations and the like. (And as Nihad Awad of CAIR says, "Mosques are not only centers for spirituality, they are now bases for political and social mobilization.")[3] Fitaihi himself, who is from a wealthy Saudi family that made its fortune in jewelry and shopping malls, is one of several influential Muslim leaders behind the construction of a new $22 million mosque and cultural center that will eventually tower above the Roxbury neighborhood of Boston and be the largest mosque in the northeast of America.

"This is a dream for generations of Muslims which is beginning to be accomplished here in the heart of the city of Boston," he was reported as saying in the *Boston Herald* in 2004. "We will build, with Allah's permission, an Islamic cultural center and we will raise the tallest minaret on a mosque in the United States."

Another of the mosque's backers is the cleric Dr. Yusuf Abdullah al-Qaradawi, a senior member of the radical Islamic Brotherhood, who preaches that while some countries of the world will come under Muslim rule through armed jihad, others, like America, will be fortunate enough to be conquered peacefully through *da'wa*, with the result that non-Muslim Americans will eventually convert to Islam in droves.

Many influential Muslims are convinced that a spiritual void of epic proportions stretches across not only much of North America, but across Western Europe as well. Furthermore, they see it as their duty to do something about it.

"There is a religious vacuum in the West, and it is el-Islam which will fill that vacuum," the most prominent imam in New York City, Omar Abu Namous, told me. "The present culture is poisonous. It poisoned the life of the world when it said that we are free. This word 'freedom' is poison. You have a master who created you, so you are a servant. How can you be free if you have a master? You are a servant. The European or the Western culture has poisoned the minds of the world because of this. Islam is going to bring the normalcy of the situation back. Islam is going to say, 'No, we are not free, we have to listen to God.'"

WHITE MUSLIM

Five days before 9/11, Charles Vincent was already listening to God, though not yet with sufficient care. On a whim, he bought his first Koran from a street vendor in Queens, and after the World Trade Center came down, he started reading it. Six weeks later, while smoke was still pouring from Ground Zero, he formally converted to Islam in the mosque attached to the Islamic Cultural Center on 96th Street and Third Avenue in New York City. A blond, blue-eyed 29-year-old from Torrance, California, he readily admits that he chose an unlikely moment to fall in love with the world's most controversial religion. But in the years since, his devotion to the faith has only deepened. Like a growing number of white Americans and Europeans elsewhere, he has discovered that Islam is not just the religion of those "other" people.

"Every day I'm more surprised than the day before," he told me one evening in October, breaking his Ramadan fast in a harshly lit fast food restaurant a few blocks from the 96th Street mosque. "The last religion I wanted to belong to was Islam. The last word that came out of my mouth was *Allah*. Islam pulled me out of the biggest hole I've ever been in."

Dressed as he is in a *thobe*, an Islamic-style tunic, and a white *kufi*, or skullcap, with an untrimmed ginger beard sprouting from his hand-some, classically Californian face, Charles may look unusual, but he certainly isn't alienated, or, for that matter, alone. In the United States, there are estimated to be something like 80,000 white and Hispanic Muslims, along with a far greater number of African-American ones. In France, there are perhaps 50,000, according to a secret government intelligence report leaked to the French newspaper *Le Figaro*. (A Muslim resident of the racially mixed Belleville district of Paris told me that out of every 100 Muslims one sees there, 30 are former French Catholics.) The report stated that conversion to Islam "has become a phenomenon [in France] that needs to be followed closely." A recent study commissioned by Jonathan ("Yahya") Birt, a Muslim convert and the son of a former director-general of the BBC, put the figure in Britain at a more modest 14,000, and there are similar estimates for Spain and Germany. More people are converting on all sides of the globe— from Australia and New Zealand to Sweden and Denmark. It has been claimed that 30,000 people have converted in Switzerland alone.[4] At the moment the number of converts can only be called a trickle, but it is steady and gathering in power.

To become a Muslim is surprisingly easy. All you need to do is take *Shahadah*—say, *Ash'hadwin la ilaha illa Allah, Ash'hadwin Muhammadur rasoolu Allah*

("I affirm there is no true God but God, and Muhammad is the Messenger of God") three times in front of a Muslim witness (or, according to some people, two witnesses) and, bingo, you're a Muslim. That done, you are expected to pray five times a day, donate a certain amount of money to charity, fast between sunrise and sunset during the month of Ramadan, and, health and finances permitting, make at least one *haj*, or pilgrimage, to Mecca in Saudi Arabia during your lifetime. Collectively, these are known as the "five pillars" of Islam.

Of course, there's the small matter of *why* a non-Muslim would first choose to convert to a religion increasingly associated with dictatorial governments, mass terrorism, videotaped beheadings and the oppression of women. One reason might be disillusionment with wall-to-wall entertainment, jaded sexuality, spiritual anomie and all the other ailments of the materialistic West. Another might be protest. Criminals often convert to Islam in jail, not just because it promises to provide them with a straightforward moral framework to live by, but also because it is implicitly seen as hostile to mainstream society, and therefore solidifies their self-image as outsiders. Likewise, becoming a radical Muslim is perhaps the most extreme act of rebellion available to a bourgeois white youth raised on the pseudo-rebellion of MTV.

Intellectuals have their reasons too. A few days after George W. Bush's re-election, *Vanity Fair* critic James Wolcott joked on his blog that, in tribute to the president's (and the Christian right's) victorious pro-religion agenda, he was going to convert to Islam, not least because "fasting during Ramadan should be wonderfully slimming, enabling me to get into the Carnaby Street paisley shirt that was a bit binding the last time I tried it on." A few days later he announced he was putting his conversion on hold following a long discussion with his editor, Graydon Carter, who had pointed out that another *Vanity Fair* writer was thinking along the same lines and two Islamic converts on the same perfumed masthead might be a bit much.

In fact, had one of the *Vanity Fair* scribes been serious about going down to the mosque to offer his services to Allah, no one there would have blinked an eye. Just a week before Wolcott posted his remarks, Heriberto Silva, a Mexican-born Catholic professor of Spanish literature at the City University of New York, took *Shahadah* and became Abdullah Silva, Muslim, during Friday prayers at the 96th Street mosque. A frail 60-year-old bundled into an old parka, a thick volume entitled *A History of the Arabs* tucked under his arm, he told me afterward that his conversion was due to three factors: A long-standing fascination with the Islamic world; the encouragement of his Muslim friends; and a desire to register a personal objection to the Iraq War.

"We see a president who is preaching about freedom and democracy, and it is not true! It is all lies!" he exclaimed. "And then I am looking for something that is real truth, and I found in Islam that truth."

Charles Vincent's conversion appears to have been a more muddled, emotional affair, but also a more dramatic one, since it took place in New York against the backdrop of 9/11. Like a lot of people who convert to Islam or any other religion, he did so after a particularly difficult period in his life in which he not only lost his "way" but also lost his job and his apartment, and, after a fight outside a nightclub, came close to losing an eye as well. He also had a good Moroccan friend— the "Mysterious Moroccan," as I came to think of him, since he wouldn't speak to me, despite frequent requests for a meeting—who strongly encouraged him to convert, and may even have insisted that he do so as a price of friendship.

Muslims are just as intrigued by Charles' transformation as anyone else. "I was making prayer in this mosque during Ramadan in November 2001," he told me, "and I could feel the brother next to me stare. After the prayers, the first thing out of his mouth was, 'How did you become a Muslim?' That was very strange to me. I didn't know how to answer him. I said, 'What do you mean, how did I become a Muslim?' And he said, 'How did you become a Muslim?

You have to have a story of how you became a Muslim.' And I realized he was right. There was a process I went through. Muslims know that it's not by chance that you come into this religion. I know that now too."

FROM SIOUXSIE
AND THE BANSHEES
TO ALLAH

Charles was born into a middle-class Catholic
family in Inglewood, California, a suburb of Los
Angeles, and grew up in nearby Torrance. He was
the eighth of eight children—all boys. After "dab-
bling" in college, he took a job as a bellman at the
Torrance Marriott, and worked his way up to the
position of auditor, which he kept for five years,
working the night shift. He enjoyed the responsibil-
ity, and the feeling of being awake in a hotel in
which everyone else was asleep. But he often asked
himself what he was doing with his life, and the

answer came: "Didn't do anything today, didn't do anything today, didn't do anything today…"

A sociable loner, he would get off work at 7 in the morning, eat in a Taco Bell on Hawthorne Boulevard in Lawndale, and sleep until 3 in the afternoon. In his free time he worked out, went swimming or surfing, and hiked in the Palos Verdes. He had ambitions to be a stage actor and took part in a local production of *Red River*, but his passion was for music. His girlfriend was obsessed with the band Danzig (a band member pulled a gun on them when they broke into the grounds of his Hollywood house), and he, in turn, was obsessed with Siouxsie and the Banshees. He waited for Siouxsie outside her hotel when she played in L.A., asked her to autograph T-shirts and pose for photographs, and would stand in the front at her concerts so he could grab her leg on stage (she let him). One night, hanging around in the lobby of her hotel, he asked if she would pose for yet another photograph, and Siouxsie decided she'd had enough. "You have one minute," she answered in an icy voice. That was the last time he saw her.

When he thought about moving to New York, his brother Mike, encouraged him. "Dude," he said, "you know what? You've already worked for Marriott for five years in this nowhere city, and now they're trying to make you work even longer hours. Just go." In 1999, Charles went. Through Marriott, he arranged to take a job at the front desk of the Marriott in Times Square, while he himself lived in a hotel in the West Village. It was an old, musty, creaky place down by the waterfront whose main claim to fame was that the survivors from the *Titanic* had been put up there in 1912. In the room next to Charles' was a transvestite. As New York beginnings go, it was classic.

But within a couple of years, Charles was in trouble. He quit the Marriott and became involved in an ill-fated pet-care business venture, which was when he met the Moroccan, whom he hired off the street. It was a chaotic time, and they soon became best friends. They spent a lot of time partying, blew all their money, and by the summer of 2001 were both out of work and had lost the apartment they'd moved into in New Jersey. For a few weeks, they were homeless.

Things got even worse after Charles and the Moroccan got into a fight with a group of men outside a nightclub in Greenwich Village. Over the phone, Charles' brother Mike told me he thought the brawl may have broken out because the Moroccan was harassing some girls coming out of the club. Charles says the Moroccan had nothing to do with it; in fact, by this time the Moroccan was already rediscovering his Islamic faith and had begun to distance himself from Charles, who would see him praying and feel bewildered.

Charles' version of the story is that he and a friend from Las Vegas, Joey, saw a girl vomiting on the sidewalk outside the club. She was tiny, and she kept vomiting and vomiting, and they couldn't believe how much was coming out of her. Joey had a camera, and they decided to take a picture. When the flash went off, the girl's boyfriend looked up and said, "You think that's funny?" "Yeah, it's funny," Charles replied. They got into a shouting match, and suddenly the boyfriend was standing in front of him, ready to fight.

It was late on a Saturday night in the Village, and hundreds of people were milling about in the street. Soon they were baying for blood. Several of

the girl's other male friends joined in, and Charles
remembers being dragged across the street and
pushed down by three men, when someone hit him
in the eye. Joey had disappeared, but the
Moroccan, who was down the block, heard the
shouts and came running over. When he saw what
was happening, he tried to defend his buddy, taking on several men by himself. Eventually the
police arrived, took one look at Charles' face and
called an ambulance: A blood sac had formed in
his eye and was starting to protrude from it.

It was after being discharged from the hospital,
wearing a big bandage on his eye, that Charles saw a
Muslim selling copies of the Koran on the street in
Queens. Recalling some of the things the Moroccan
had been telling him about it, he bought one,
though he didn't read it straight away. A couple of
days later he began to lose vision in his eye. It had
become infected, and in order to prevent the infec-
tion from endangering the vision in his other eye,
the doctors told him they might have to take it out.

Shortly before 9/11, Charles ended up
spending two nights at St. Vincent's Hospital on

the west side of Manhattan, with both of his eyes bandaged, wondering if he was about to go blind. "All I could hear was the beeping of the machinery around me and the people and the nurses talking, and I guess in the darkness I had time to think about myself and my situation," he told me, recalling his frame of mind at the time.

"Where did I go wrong? I came from a good family in California—what led me to this? You know, bringing me all the way to New York to be sitting in a hospital. Here I am, I'm going to lose my eyeball. How did this happen? Why would this happen to me? And while I was covered, while I had the bandages on, that's when I prayed for the first time in my life. I asked God to not let this happen to me. And so I did a heartfelt prayer to God."

Charles' prayer appears to have been answered. The following morning the doctors took the bandages off his eyes, and the vision in his bad eye had returned. He was then rushed into the operating room for some laser surgery. By 9/11 he was out of the hospital, though still wearing a patch on his eye, and staying in a house in Queens belonging to his Moroccan friend's cousin.

The Moroccan's mother had come to visit from Casablanca, and so when the planes struck the Twin Towers, Charles—unlike most Americans—experienced the day from the perspective of someone living in the bosom of an Arab family.

"All we had to do was look out our door to see the World Trade Center, all the smoke," Charles said. "I remember being at a grocery store a block from our house, calming [the Moroccan] down. And he gave me the scenarios of how Islam was going to be the victim of all this. And again, not knowing anything about it, I said, 'Okay, calm down, calm down, I know what you're saying...'

"Because he's Arab he knew a lot of Arabs, and the Arabs he knew I knew. It was strange to see the reaction in the wee hours of this. They all knew exactly what had happened and the way it was going. They were more shocked than anybody, and they didn't know how to take me now. So the focus was on me. 'What do *you* think happened? What do *you* think about this? What do *you* think is going to happen?' I said, 'Listen, I don't know any more than you about this, so don't...' I couldn't answer any kind of question like that."

In the days after the attack, while New York's traumatized citizens stared at their television sets, watching endless replays of the planes slicing through the World Trade Center, Charles read the Koran, becoming more and more enraptured by it as he went on.

"In the second chapter it says, 'In this book you'll find no doubt,'" he told me. "Meaning no contradictions. There's nothing that's going to say one thing here and another thing there. But as you read, you understand this was not written by a man. There's a clear, clear distinction between this book and others. What was also shocking was that it clarified the other book—the Bible. It's spoken of in the Koran, and spoken of *highly* in the Koran. So I was absolutely baffled that this book I had no idea existed was explaining my book for me.

"It was a very strange time to decide to come into a religion like this," he concluded, "but for me it was meant to be. It was meant for me to see this, and it was my time to see it."

GOING IMMIGRANT

I first met Charles outside a small Bangladeshi mosque on First Avenue and 11th Street in New York's East Village. It was a Saturday night in October, and he was standing in front of the entrance talking to another Muslim, Raul ("Omar") Pacheco, a 43-year-old Spaniard who converted in his 20s and later spent five years on a scholarship in Saudi Arabia. Charles wore the Islamic dress of many of the Bangladeshis who go to the same mosque, and the light above the doorway illuminated his pale skin and blond beard.

The lines around his eyes seemed unusually pronounced for a man not yet 30. His face looked drawn, but he smiled broadly, displaying a glistening row of white, orthodontically perfect Southern Californian teeth. He said he drove a cab—like so many other Muslims. Laughing, he told me that he had converted just before 9/11— "Great timing, right?"—though the next time I saw him he had subtly amended his story, saying that at that point he had only gone so far as to purchase a Koran. I asked for his phone number, but he seemed reluctant to give it to me. His line was being tapped by the FBI, he said, like those (he claimed) of most Muslims. Instead, he gave me his e-mail address.

My impression that night was that Charles took Islam very, very seriously, almost to the point of parody. That he drove a cab seemed a bit much—it was as if he were trying to replicate a certain kind of Muslim lifestyle in America down to the last detail, to become just another Yemeni or Pakistani driving busy Westerners around. It was the reverse of the old expat, colonial phenomenon of "going native." Charles had "gone immigrant";

he'd expatriated himself inside his own country. (At times, he even spoke like an immigrant. "Thanks God for Islam," he would often say, rather than, "Thank God.") There was something moving about his sincerity. Was he learning Arabic? Did he plan to go to Mecca? Was he still in touch with his old friends from L.A. and elsewhere? What did his parents think? Had the FBI talked to him? There wasn't time to ask. Explaining that he was working the night shift in his cab, Charles excused himself and disappeared into the darkness.

Omar, it turned out, taught Arabic at the mosque on 96th Street, and he told me that for a while Charles had been one of his pupils. Unlike Charles, he was dressed in conventional street clothes. Looking at him, no one would have guessed he was a Muslim. He looked like an ordinary Spaniard of the Almodóvar generation, and had a Texan wife—also a Muslim. ("My wife is a cowboy!" he joked.) His own preference was for the Sufi branch of Islam, which he believed was less doctrinaire, more poetic in its essence than the dominant Sunni brand.

And what did he think of Charles? "I was like that once," he responded, adding that he also had worn the white *kufi* and Arab dress. But now he no longer felt the need to advertise his Muslim status. "Ninety percent of the Europeans who have embraced Islam went through a certain kind of crisis, of not being completely satisfied," he told me. "I was very indecisive and unfocused when I was young, and Islam brought me steadfastness, energy. It makes sense, Islam. There are many crazy people, of course."

It was over a week before I saw Charles again, but a few days later I met Omar up at the 96th Street mosque, where he had invited me to look in on an Arabic class he was teaching. The class room was tiny, one in a series of partitioned cubicles running along one side of the downstairs prayer room, which was lined with exquisite blue tiles. There was space for only a handful of students. One, a Sufi Muslim who I'll call "George,"was a white, 58-year-old professor of business management, a scholarly looking Vietnam veteran who wore half-glasses and an old, comfortable sweater.

The other pupils were an African-American couple and their three boys. The father, who spoke frequently in class, seemed to take it for granted that the lesson was at least as much about Islam as it was about learning Arabic.

Omar was dressed in a gray suit, with just a sports shirt underneath—and of course, no shoes: Everyone who got past the entrance of the mosque was either barefoot or in socks. His socks were white, which rather ruined the effect of the suit. He was a patient teacher, blessed with preternaturally calm blue eyes that gazed into your own so frankly it could be unnerving. The three boys, dressed in baggy jeans and brightly colored football shirts, dutifully copied the sentences he wrote on the blackboard, but they seemed to be afflicted with attention deficit disorder. They stuck their heads inside their shirts and made abrupt, jerky movements in their seats. The youngest boy sneezed repeatedly, drawing a mild reproof from Omar. "When you are sick, you are not supposed to come to the mosque," he informed him gently.

I wondered what Omar thought of his pupils. He had told me this was a beginner-intermediate class, but it was hard to believe that anyone in it would ever attain enough knowledge of Arabic even to order a sandwich or buy a train ticket, let alone read the Koran. It was as if the lesson were a symbol of the attempt to learn Arabic (a notoriously complex language) rather than the attempt itself. The examples Omar used to teach with were mainly taken from the sayings (*hadiths*) of Muhammad. One *hadith* in the exercise book, highlighting the Prophet's enlightened views on women, read as follows:

> The prophet said to me:
> "Hand me over the mat from the mosque."
> I said, "I am menstruating."
> He said: "Thy menses are not in thy hand."

While the lesson went on, worshipers went in and out of the prayer room. A few wore traditional Islamic clothing, but most looked as if they had just gotten out of their cabs or delivery vans, which in fact they had, to stop by for a quick prayer. Some even wore baseball caps. It wasn't an official prayer time, and people stood or sat in their own spaces, directing their thoughts toward Mecca without a trace of self-consciousness before rushing back to their cars. In New York, Christians could no longer just drop in on a church when the spirit moved them and spend a few contemplative moments in a pew, because churches were only open for services. The Muslim freedom to visit a mosque at any time of day and well into the evening was enviable, as was the freedom to stand, sit, lie, kneel, read or simply lounge. In the far corner of the room, two young men lay face-to-face on the carpet and murmured to each other like lovers in a field. What were they discussing? It was anyone's guess.

Omar went over an Arabic sentence he had just put on the blackboard: "The Muslim is he from whose tongue and hand the Muslim is safe."

"What does that mean?" asked one of the boys.

"It means a real Muslim will use his tongue— his speech—honorably, and also his hands—his action. In other words, if I behave dishonorably, I am not a Muslim in this case."

Another sentence read: "The seeking of universal knowledge is incumbent to every Muslim, male or female." In other words, said Omar, "To keep the woman in the kitchen is not going to work. Universal knowledge means for man and woman both."

Noble sentiments, but the women in the mosque were a minor, barely visible presence. They had their own balcony in the huge upstairs prayer room, but that was used only on Fridays. Downstairs they were provided with a small space curtained off from the men. As I was leaving the mosque at the end of the class, I was surprised to see one young African-American woman dressed head to toe in black, with her hair and face covered. Her eyes looked beautiful, though.

Ten days after our first encounter, I arranged to meet Charles outside the 11th Street mosque at around 1:30 on a Thursday afternoon. Even allowing for the fact that it was Ramadan, the number of people filing in and out would have astonished a priest, who would have been over-joyed to have that many congregants in a week.

There were plenty of churches, even a cathedral
(since demolished) nearby, but most of them were
locked. Whereas there were about 100 people in
the mosque, as many as it could fit, with rows and
rows of barefoot men listening to a pre-recorded
voice intone prayers in Arabic.

At 1:45, Charles pulled up in his cab and
apologized for being late—he'd had to take
someone to the airport. He was wearing dark,
almost-wraparound glasses that made him look
like a postmodern American ayatollah, a hip blind
sheikh. He was sniffling because of a cold and
limping because of a pinched nerve in his back.
On his wrist he wore a chunky Swatch wrist-
watch—a gift from the Moroccan. I asked if I
could take his photograph, but he said he would
prefer it if I didn't. (He later allowed photographs
to be taken.) It's against the true Muslim's belief,
he claimed, as is shaking hands with a woman
other than one's wife. Movies are now forbidden as
well, as is music, because Muhammad said it was
"of the devil." In his cab, Charles either listened
to the news or to Arabic-language tapes. The last

time he was back home in California, he'd gathered up his entire music collection—CDs, records, rare LPs he'd hunted down on Melrose Avenue, videos of concerts, rock star posters, jars of ticket stubs from concerts by Siouxsie and the Banshees, Danzig, Ministry, Lollapalooza, Sisters of Mercy, Christian Death, etc. —and dumped the whole lot into an industrial-size garbage can in his mother's back garden. And felt really good about it too. It was as if he'd purged himself of a lifetime of Western culture.

"Why shouldn't you listen to music?" I asked.

"Because it takes up valuable space in my mind, space I need for the entire Koran rather than Michael Jackson's 'Beat It' or something nonsensical like that. These things are not going to benefit me in the hereafter, they will only be held against me."

Mateen Siddiqui, vice president of the Michigan-based Islamic Supreme Council of America (ISCA), a Sufi Muslim organization that has many white adherents and keeps tabs on fundamentalist Islam in America, calls that "a very hardcore, Taliban-style belief. I wouldn't say it's

militant, but it's very extreme. The problem is it
can often lead to a militant attitude in the future."
According to the ISCA, the majority of mosques
in the United States have been taken over by radi-
cals who preach the dour, restrictive Wahhabi
Islam financed and championed by Saudi Arabia.

"If you go to an ordinary Islamic country,"
Siddiqui told me, "they don't act like that. Most
Muslims watch TV, take pictures, listen to
music.... The same is true of a lot of the people
who go to the mosques in America. The people who
go to them are normal Muslims, but the people who
run them are very strict. If a new Muslim comes,
they will grab him and indoctrinate him."

Had something like this happened to Charles?
In *The Two Faces of Islam*, a study of Wahhabism,
Stephen Schwartz discusses another Californian
convert, the notorious "American Taliban" John
Walker Lindh, who was captured in Afghanistan,
apparently waging jihad against his country.
"The speed with which he succumbed to Wahhabi
conditioning is seen in his peremptory rejection of
music almost as soon as he began praying and

studying—not just hip-hop music, with its negative and arguably destructive character, but all music," writes Schwartz, who thought that Lindh's conversion was partly a product of his own superficial culture and existence. "Wahhabism filled the emptiness in Lindh exactly as 'militia' paranoia filled the void in homegrown American terrorist Timothy McVeigh," he argues.

The rejection of music also played a role in the religious development of another young convert from California, Adam "Yahiye" Gadahn, now on the FBI's "Most Wanted" list. A fan of "death metal" bands like Cannibal Corpse and Hellbound, in 1993 Gadahn contributed music reviews and artwork to a 'zine called Xenocide. "Autopsy's newest and sickest! Eighteen tracks to mangle your mind!" he wrote in a review of *Acts of the Unspeakable* released on the Vile label. "The Bay Area quartet crank it up to a good fast grind on many of these tunes, notably 'Tortured Moans of Agony,' 'Battery Acid Enema,' 'Blackness Within' and 'Skullptures'.... This is an excellent release from some Death Metal pioneers!"

Similar accolades flowed from Gadahn's pen for an EP released by the band General Surgery: "This is basically a Swedish 'supergroup' of death, featuring members of Dismember, Afflicted and Creamatory.... Lyrically, the quote on the back cover pretty much sums it up: 'Murder is the only way to kill time.'"

In 1995, Gadahn began studying Islam at the Islamic Society of Orange County, whose imam, Muzammil Siddiqi, had shared the stage with President Bush during the 9/11 memorial service at Washington National Cathedral. The other men in Gadahn's study group were young fundamentalists, mostly Pakistanis, who spent hours at the mosque praying together in a circle. They spoke to others in a way that was reported to be "rigid" and "cruel," and they vehemently criticized other Muslims at the mosque for supposed religious laxity. In particular, they targeted the mosque's chairman, Haitham "Danny" Bundakji, for wearing Western clothes and being overly friendly with Jews. They called him "Danny the Jew."[5]

It was around this time that Gadahn posted a statement on the University of Southern California's website entitled "Becoming Muslim." He described the death metal music he had once championed as "demonic," and scolded himself for having lived a life devoted to nothing more than expanding his record collection. Sounding like a sheepish teenager (he was 18 at the time), he apologized for having annoyed his parents, for having "eschewed personal cleanliness" and for leaving his room at home in a permanent state of disarray.

He also spoke of his conversion, which came about through repeated visits to Islamic web sites on the fledgling Internet. "I discovered that the beliefs and practices of [Islam] fit my personal theology and intellect as well as basic human logic," he wrote. "Islam presents God not as an anthropomorphic being but as an entity beyond human comprehension, transcendent of man, independent and undivided." The religion's lack of hierarchy particularly seemed to appeal to him. "Islam has a holy book that is comprehensible to a layman, and there is no papacy or priesthood that is considered infallible in matters of interpretation," he wrote approvingly. "All Muslims are free to reflect and interpret the book given a sufficient education."

In May 1997, an increasingly radical and angry Gadahn was arrested for attacking the mosque's chairman. (He slapped him with an open hand.) He was charged with a misdemeanor assault and spent two days in jail. Two years later he informed his parents he was moving to Pakistan and disappeared until he suddenly showed up on the FBI's "Most Wanted" list for plotting terrorist acts against the United States. Shortly before the presidential election of November 2004, an al-Qaeda-style videotape was released to the American news media in which a masked young man, thought to be Gadahn, threatened to make the streets of America "run with blood." Like that other Californian convert, John Walker Lindh, his accent seemed to have taken on a self-conscious Arabic coloring during his time abroad. Shortly before the fourth anniversary of 9/11, another tape was released in which Gadahn praised the "echo of explosions and the slitting of the throats of the infidels" and predicted a massive al-Qaeda attack on Los Angeles and Melbourne, among other places, "Allah willing." No one knows if Gadahn—if it really is Gadahn—is working alone or in cooperation with al-Qaeda, or indeed if he is a terrorist at all. Likewise, it is still not clear whether John Walker Lindh was deliberately fighting against his own country or whether he was simply a confused young man who swallowed an alien ideology whole and wound up stuck in a muddy Afghan trench on the opposing side.

Charles, who for the most part struck me as an extremely enthusiastic devotee of his new religion rather than a militant or fanatic—he often talked about Islam with such ardor you'd have thought he was talking about a girl he was madly in love with—denied that he had been manipulated by anyone in the mosques he went to, or by his Arab acquaintances. On the contrary, he said that he and his Moroccan friend discovered— rediscovered in the latter's case—Islam and the

Koran together. But his interpretation of Islam
was clearly of the Wahhabi-fundamentalist type,
and hostile to anything less hard-edged.

"Be careful of that stuff," he told me in his kindly way when the topic of Sufism, a mystical branch of the religion disliked by orthodox Muslims, came up during one of our first conversations. A frown furrowed his brow. "I'll just give you a little example of what I mean by that. The Prophet Muhammad, *salla 'alayhi wa sallam* [peace and blessings be upon him], anything that came out of his mouth was recorded, just like you're recording now. And he said this religion will break up into 73 sects, and all of them are going into the hellfire except for the one on the true path of true religion. So when it comes to Sufism, it's not anything I would consider to be…For me, I can't consider that being any part of an article about Islam."

"So you consider yourself a Sunni Muslim?"

"I would say I was a Muslim following the one true path."

ISLAM IS A
WAY OF LIFE

While Charles worshiped inside the small
Bangladeshi mosque on 11th Street, facing a wall
decorated with a map of the Muslim world and
five clocks displaying the different prayer times,
a small, bearded man in traditional Islamic
costume approached me on the sidewalk. His
brown eyes were wide open, unblinking, con-
sciously mesmeric, and a big smile lit up his face.
Did I have any questions? Was there anything I
wanted to know about Islam? He said his name
was Hesham el-Ashry, that he was an Egyptian

from Cairo, and he invited me to sit down with him on the mosque's carpeted floor to talk.

Nearby people were praying, sitting around, chatting quietly, even—in the case of one African-American—stretched out asleep. One saw this often in mosques, which are open all day long and well into the evening. In New York, a Muslim who is weary or has a few hours to kill can walk into the nearest mosque, take off his shoes and make himself comfortable, whether he's in midtown Manhattan or one of the boroughs. The day's five formal prayer services punctuate the day rather than define it. In mosques, the praying never stops.

There was a small curtained area for women to worship in, but I didn't see any women. Someone later explained that this was due to the fact that women are not required to go to the mosque as often as men, and since the majority of Muslim immigrants are male, there are less women anyway. Nonetheless, the overall impression one receives in the mosques is that women are treated, if not as second-class citizens exactly, then almost as an afterthought. In fact, watching the men go in and out of this one little mosque—a thousand or so per day—one might easily mistake it for a

kind of social club for men.

According to Saraji Umm Zaid, a female convert and writer who is the webmaster for *modernmuslima.com*, *sunnisisters.com* and *iprofess.com* (a website for converts), many American mosques bar women from praying on the grounds that there isn't sufficient room to maintain a separate area for them. In an essay entitled "Why Every Mosque Should be Woman-Friendly," Zaid wrote that "Because the Prophet Muhammad specifically forbade keeping women from the mosque, no one is going to come right out and say that they bar women from entering. 'We don't have room' becomes code for 'We don't want you here. Go home.'" The result, she continued, is that "a multitude of viewpoints, ideas, and energy have been eliminated. More than 50 percent of the local community becomes invisible and excluded.... Is this the public face of our *da'wa* (the invitation to Islam)? A face that is exclusively male? How can we tell non-Muslim women that Islam is a sheltering place for them if we show them a community in which women are virtually invisible?"[6]

Zaid is obviously a sophisticated, well-educated woman who knows her American rights. On a Latino Muslim web site for converts can be found a rather remarkable document in which one Rocio Martinez-Mendoza, a Mexican who immigrated to Texas and converted following her marriage to a Moroccan man, gives an account of her *haj* to Mecca, complete with downloaded snapshots of mosques and minarets and thronged processional streets.... It is the timid yet gutsy way in which she describes her reactions to Saudi society that suggests that Islam won't be able to continue playing by the old sexist, statist rules in America forever. Though she obviously loved the experience of the *haj* proper, and reveled in all the holy places she visited, she could not help noticing the number and disgraceful condition of the beggars; the vast gulf between rich and poor; the entirely submissive position of the women; and most damningly, perhaps, the way the Saudis themselves seemed to do no work at all other than "resting in the street and smoking." (In fact, it appeared to her that Bangladeshi guest workers did all the work, and were none too well treated for their

labors.) All in all, it doesn't seem terribly "Islamic"
to the Latina from Texas who nonetheless ends her
newsletter by humbly begging forgiveness in case
her observations should have offended anyone.[7]

It's unlikely that el-Ashry was very concerned
with either the plight of women in mosques or
what a Muslim convert in the United States might
think about life in Saudi Arabia.

"Thanks be to Allah, that he made me Muslim,"
he began, warming up with a brief homily on the
"five pillars" of Islam. His English was good, if
eccentric, and he had a honey-smooth voice. "We
are not Muslims because we are wise, we are not
Muslims because we are clever, we are not Muslims
because we are so smart. Even when we worship,
when we come to pray, when we fast, it is a blessing
from Allah. He pleases us by making us Muslims,
and by making us worship him."

"Why did you come to the United States?"
I asked.

El-Ashry smiled enigmatically. Perhaps it was
a question he had often heard, or perhaps it was a

question no one ever asked him. "The reason is coming to work, to stay here, to have a better life—like everybody. But then afterward I learned that my traveling from my home country to any other place should be, first of all, to make *da'wa*—to tell people about what is Islam, the truth of Islam, the reality of Islam. So I changed my intentions, and I made my main purpose [in] America to talk about Islam, and my second purpose, to work and make a living."

El-Ashry estimates that he has converted about 20 white Americans to Islam, though he believes that you don't "convert" to Islam, you "revert" to it, since we are all Muslim at birth—to become Muslim is simply to return to one's natural state. (As Charles said to me, even dogs and cats are Muslim, since they behave exactly as Allah decrees. When I reported this remark to author Stephen Schwartz, himself a convert—though a vastly more learned one—he replied contemptuously: "How then to explain the Islamic arguments against keeping them as pets? This guy has the typical Lindh habit of claiming authority about things he knows nothing of. Very common among 'Wahoo' converts. In the words of the

Prophet, 'Islam passes through them as an arrow
through the body of an animal.'") The Americans
he converted, said el-Ashry, had lots of questions
about Islam, from why Muslims "kiss the ground"
five times a day to why they encircle a black box in
the desert. "So when I explained the truth and the
reality about everything, then they found out
things that completely changed their idea about
Islam. They found out the truth about Islam, and
about 20 of them asked, 'Can we be Muslims?'
And I said, 'Well, you have to be Muslims.'"

I asked how many Americans he thought
would convert to Islam in the future.

"Only Allah knows that. I wish all would
be Muslims."

"How did you meet these Americans?"

"You see the way I met you?" el-Ashry replied.
"People be looking at me with a critical eye, sometimes. Sometimes they stop me in the street, talking.
Sometimes my neighbors. Sometimes the people
I'm working with. Wherever I have a connection
with people. And sometimes people come to the
mosque, asking questions, and I talk to them."

I asked el-Ashry about the way Muslims pray, the different positions they adopt—sitting, standing up, bending down with hands on knees, head down on the floor.

"We pray, or we are supposed to pray, in the same way the Prophet Muhammad prayed," he explained. "He said, 'Pray in the same way you see me pray.' So that's why we have to do every single movement according to what he used to do. He taught us where to look, how to stand, where to put your hands, how to open your legs or close your legs. Every single thing he taught us how to do. And this is not only in the prayers, because what people doesn't know about Islam is [that] it's not a religion."

"What is it then?"

"Islam is a way of life. The Prophet Muhammad, peace be upon him, taught us everything up to how to go to the bathroom. Even when you go to the bathroom, how to go in, how to go out, how to sit, how to wash, how to take a shower. [He taught us] how to eat, how to start your food, how to treat your wife, how to treat your children,

how to wake up in the morning, how to put your
slippers on, how to put clothes on, how to take
clothes off, what to eat, what not to eat…And
everything had a purpose."

TAXI DRIVER

Presumably the Prophet Muhammad, peace and blessings be upon him, did not leave written instructions on how a Muslim should drive a cab in New York City. Even Charles, with his long experience in the ultimate car culture of Southern California, said he had had to learn to be more aggressive in order to survive in the streets of Manhattan. As Charles saw it, Islam had not only granted him a new name—Shu'aib ("Think of 'shoe' and 'Abe' Lincoln," he suggested helpfully)— it had also made him into a completely different person than the happy-go-lucky one known to his friends and family back in Torrance. Even to himself.

"In L.A., I had no direction. I was absolutely clueless as to what I was going to do for the rest of my life. I really cared mostly about the irrelevant things—my music, my hanging out, my friends, my parties. Anything that had no weight or relevance to it, that was what I was most concerned about. I was working just like anybody, living for the weekend, to buy clothes, impress myself, impress others.

"What I can tell you is this," he went on, his voice hoarse and nasal because of his cold, his throat dry from fasting. (It was already seven hours since his last meal.) "There was Charles, and there's Shu'aib. And literally it's two different people. Why? Because I could never, God willing, be that person again. Meaning my character, my mentality, my closed eyes, my narrowmindedness—everything was just wrong. I use the analogy that I had to have my vision taken away from me to have my eyes opened. All I can say is thanks God for Islam, because it teaches you everything about this life, about this world. It makes you ponder everything, not in a spiritual kind of way, but in a reality kind of way. So when I see things—"

"What do you see *here*, for example?" I asked as we sped uptown on a beautiful fall day past stores selling expensive jewelry and the finest clothing, past a stunning Japanese woman waiting at the light in a long white coat, her white poodle, straining on the leash, in a coat as well.

"Only God knows what's in people's hearts, and how they really are and how they really feel, but what I see is a lot of people who are misguided," Charles said, frowning behind the wheel. "Where are they going? What are they doing? What are their objectives today? Did they stop today to say thanks God for these new clothes I'm wearing? Did they stop today to say thanks God for the food they ate? Did they stop to call their parents? That's what I see people lacking."

Shu'aib's life was far more demanding than the one Charles lived in the past, and he drove himself far harder than the average Muslim. Every day he rose before dawn, washed (and, during Ramadan, ate), before hurrying down to the 96th Street mosque for the morning prayer, usually in the company of 40 or 50 sleepy worshipers. By 5 a.m., he was in his cab, which he picked up at a depot on 86th Street and Lexington Avenue. The streets were dark, the air frigid. For the next 12 hours he was both in control and controlled by others—a driver at the mercy of his passengers. The city was dotted with mosques, and he had to find one of them to pray in at lunch time (though he wouldn't eat) and again in the middle of the afternoon before finally turning in his cab at 5 p.m. On an average day his take was $85, and he didn't seem to mind how hard he had to work for it. "In Islam, money is nothing," he said with a trace of contempt. "We don't wake up in the morning with dollar signs in our eyes. The first thing we do in the morning is pray."

Four nights a week, he went to night school at LaGuardia Community College in Queens, where he took classes in anthropology, the Bible as literature, and Western civilization. He has also served as the vice president and president of the college's

Muslim Students Association, which he helped organize with Avais, a good-humored Pakistani student with a thick mop of black hair. Last year, Charles gave a talk entitled "How Islam Changed Me" for the student association. "We wanted to show that he's a Muslim and that he's part of our family—to make a statement that Muslims are not always South Asian or Arab," Avais told me one evening, while he, Charles and a handful of other Muslim men, including a Jewish-born New Yorker who was also a convert, were breaking fast in a room above a mosque on 55th Street. The atmosphere was convivial and collegiate. "It's time to pig out," one of the party joked, digging into his food. Then, humorously alluding to the Muslim prohibition on pork, he corrected himself: "Maybe I should say, 'Cow out.'"

Charles' talk was a success. Afterward, a white student in the audience named Eric, now Farouk, came into Islam. Within a year Eric had converted his mother, sister and grandmother, Charles said, sounding a mite envious. (He longed to convert his parents, even daydreamed about it while he was in his cab, with an intensity that might have startled his mother, who, much as she respected her son's choice, told me she had no intention of joining an organized faith.) The college had a sizable Muslim population, and the non-Muslim students were intrigued by Islam. Charles got a lot of inquiries, often from girls, who, to show off their interfaith sophistication, would start a conversation with him by saying, "Oh, I know somebody who is an Islamer," or "I know someone who believes in Muslims."

From the outside, Charles' life could look a little grim. He drove a cab—a job white Americans outsourced long ago to Third World immigrants. He had no health insurance and, despite a serious back problem, had been going to a doctor popular with cabdrivers who sounded like something out of a William Burroughs novel. A reputable physician won't give you a back injection without having an MRI taken first, but Charles got four back injections and a bottle of painkillers within two visits. ("Where does it hurt?" the doctor asked, prodding his spine before plunging in the needle.) The painkillers helped, but they made him dopey too—which, on top of the lack of food and water and punishing sleep schedule (near the end of Ramadan, he spent a night praying in the mosque and then went straight to work), hardly made him the ideal driver from a passenger's point of view. As for women, not only did he not have a girlfriend, he wasn't even permitted to touch a female hand. He hoped to get married, but his wife would either have to be Muslim or willing to convert immediately. "Women are just part of this life," he told me. "They're just part of this world. So they're not going to be beneficial to you in any way. I'm not speaking of Muslim women. I'm speaking of regular women on the street. In my opinion, *they're* the ones who are oppressed, not the Muslim women. Ask any Muslim woman if she's oppressed, and they're going to say no. They wouldn't be fighting like they are with this head-scarf issue in France—you know why? Because they don't *want* to take it off. Why would they upset the Creator, rather than the Creation? They're not going to let the Creation ordain for them what the Creator has already ordained.

"For sisters, now, they get utmost respect. Not just from Shu'aib but from any Muslim brother. Ask any Muslim brother, and he'll tell you that just by seeing a scarf on a woman's face, on her hair, they have nothing but respect for her. They cannot disrespect this person. Why? Because she's doing what was ordained for her to do—which is cover herself, have modesty. She's following what was God's orders."

A woman not following God's orders flagged us down from the curb. Wrapped in a fashionably cut red coat, she was in her 40s, brisk and business-like, with lips that were two thin crimson lines. "Sixty-second and Madison," she ordained, getting into the cab for a five-block ride.

"Where is she going, what is she doing?" Charles asked after she got out a few minutes later. "To me, the way I see it now, people are living and dying for this world. So much so that nothing else matters, nothing else is relevant. What is relevant is the bag in her hand. She needs to make sure she looks good, that she's up to par. She needs to spend her money on...nonsense! To me, and

from being Muslim, I don't need any of this.
I don't need to waste my time with these people,
because they're not here for the same purpose I'm
here for, they don't see things the way I see them.
They're running very fast, and what's going to
happen at the end? They're going to die!"

Such predictable talk ought to have sounded
robotic, but Charles had a way of making even the
most programmed religious remarks sound as
fresh as if they had been conceived that morning.
He was that very particular thing, a fully-fledged
convert brimfull with all the convert's passionate
conviction, and for the most part his comments
sounded warm and heartfelt rather than disparaging
and contemptuous.

Heading down the FDR Drive, with the East
River streaming past us on our left, the conversation turned to politics. It was a week or so before
the 2004 presidential election, but Charles said he
had no intention of voting. Democracy is based
on compromise, he asserted, and Islam does
not compromise. If he could vote for an Islamic
state, he would, with Saudi Arabia as the model.

I was reminded of a lecture on Islam, delivered by an Egyptian professor in Doha, Qatar in the late 1970s, which the great English travel writer Jonathan Raban wrote about in his book, *Arabia: A Journey through the Labyrinth.* "Islam is a societistic, not an individualistic religion," the professor had said. "It is continually on the move toward a social ethic, toward the idea of Islam as a state—a federal union of communities built on Islamic Law."

Asked about Taliban-era Afghanistan, Charles replied cautiously that he didn't know enough about it to comment. It was his fervent hope that before long, in the company of a million or so other Muslims, he would be able to go on the *haj* and circle the black stone at Mecca. "Besides wanting my parents to become Muslim, there's nothing I want more."

THE SYRIAN
ISLAM-SPREADER

The floor of the men's room in the 96th Street mosque was awash in water. To the left of the entrance stood a huge basket of mismatched flip-flops and sandals, to be put on before going inside. Along one wall men sat on marble blocks in front of taps for people to perform their *wudu'*—ritual ablutions—washing feet, arms up to the elbow, rinsing nose and eyes—in preparation for prayer. There were no urinals, just a row of cubicles complete with a tap on one side (for more ablutions) and a plastic bucket on the other. Talking in the men's room is strongly discouraged. Achieving cleanliness before God is a serious business.

It was Friday prayers. One Muslim among many, Charles found a place on the vast carpeted floor of the main prayer room, and was soon swallowed up by the crowd. Topped by a copper dome, angled 29 degrees off the New York street grid in order to face Mecca, the mosque was designed by the architectural firm of Skidmore, Owings and Merrill and opened offically in September, 1991. Inside it felt light and airy and immensely comfortable, like the world's biggest yoga studio. There was an upstairs balcony for the "sisters," as well as a *mihrab*—a kind of understated altar—and a *minbar*, or pulpit, an upright latticed box at the top of five carpeted steps from which the imam delivered the *khutba*, or sermon. There were no pews, no chairs, no furniture of any kind at all—just an immense plush carpet, a calming green with geometric splashes of color, large enough to accommodate several tennis courts. With its informality and stretches of empty space, the mosque could make a church or a cathedral look pointlessly elaborate and ornate, and it felt

curiously modern and user-friendly.

Except during specific prayer times, you don't
have to be silent in a mosque, and if a cell phone
goes off, nobody makes a fuss. On the contrary,
two people can sit and talk while, nearby, someone
else prays. Furthermore, the sense of a strict
beginning and end to the service is lacking. It is
nothing like a church service where, at a certain
point, the priest begins and someone shuts the
doors. For Muslims, it appears to be perfectly
acceptable to arrive on time, or 10, 20, 30 or even
40 minutes late. The effect of this is to create a
sense of endlessness, of wave after wave of
arrivals. The mosque's already perilous margins—
the thin bands of unoccupied space along the
walls—eventually disappear, as do all aisles or
obvious escape routes. For a non-Muslim, it can
feel quite claustrophobic.

By 1:30 or so, the mosque, both upstairs and
down, was packed to overflowing, which meant
there were several thousand people there with
more lining up outside. (Carpets had been laid out

in the grounds to accommodate those who couldn't get in, and a mountain of castoff shoes had been formed outside the front door.) A slender young woman, veiled in unusually filmy black, rushed in through a side entrance, slipping off a pair of silver-mesh slippers before continuing barefoot on her way up to the balcony. The shoes were inlaid with a beaded flower pattern, and the label on the insole said "SWEET." Lying on the marble floor, inches from the carpet, they looked deliciously sinful.

Sheikh Muhammad al-Yaqoubi, a Syrian preacher with green eyes, milk-white skin, a bulbous, almost muscular forehead and a cunning face framed by a bushy ginger beard (people at the mosque joked that he and Charles were brothers) ascended the stairs to the pulpit to deliver the sermon. Charles had heard al-Yaqoubi before and approved. "He's pretty blunt," he told me, suggesting that the Syrian, unlike some preachers, wasn't afraid to speak his mind. Al-Yaqoubi wore a white hat that looked like a tassel-less fez, and a long, pale, hooded Moroccan robe. Holding a pair of black worry beads in one hand, clutching the stair railing with the other, he made a strikingly archaic and authoritative figure. For a while he spoke in Arabic, then switched to English.

Al-Yaqoubi, who spends every Ramadan at the New York mosque but is also a regular visitor to California (he teaches in both Orange County and at the Zaytuna Institute in the Bay Area), is what might be termed an itinerant Islam-spreader. Based in Damascus, Syria, he traces his lineage back to the Prophet and is the son of the celebrated Syrian scholar, Sheikh Ibrahim al-Yaqoubi. As a small boy, he played in the Grand Umayyad Mosque and the Darwishiyya Mosque, where his father taught for 40 years. Al-Yaqoubi himself taught his first class on the Koran at the age of 11 and delivered his first *khutba* at the age of 14. He is a classically trained Islamic scholar of a kind one rarely comes across in the United States. He studied *Shari'a*—the code of law based on the Koran—at the University of Damascus, has a degree in Arabic Literature from the University of Beirut, and has studied extensively in the fields of philosophy and linguistics. He was the imam in a mosque in Gothenberg, Sweden, for several years. In 1999, he was appointed Mufti (an Islamic scholar who interprets *Shari'a* law) of Sweden by the Swedish Islamic Society in Stockholm, and he has lectured and preached in England, Canada, Scotland, Switzerland, Germany, France, Spain, Denmark, Finland, Norway and the United States, as well as in many Arab countries. He speaks Arabic, English and Swedish, reads French and German, and lectures on everything from the great Sufi poet Rumi to the finer points of *Shari'a* law. He has been to the United States more than 25 times since 1997, and, given the cost of the average flight between New York and Damascus, not to mention Stockholm and Edinburgh and Strasbourg and L.A., someone must be funding him handsomely.

The theme of his sermon, which was entitled "The Ongoing Battle—But Who Is the Enemy?," was jihad, an Arabic word which means "struggle." The Koran talks about jihad in three different ways, he said. The first is jihad as war, whether in self-defense when a Muslim country is attacked, or the spreading of Islam by force—a form of jihad which, he told me later, "most speakers try to run away from, they become apologetic." The second major category of jihad is preaching—the peaceful dissemination of Islamic civilization, wisdom, and principles. Lastly was the most personal form of jihad, the one that goes on every day of a Muslim's life—the battle with the self, with the ego, with temptation.

Although this was one of the largest and best-known mosques in the United States, and therefore presumably a showcase for the acceptable face of Islam in America, the sermon was both moderate and inflammatory in tone, switching from one to the other almost sentence by sentence. But when you listened to it closely, even the "moderate" parts often sounded like veiled threats.

"Anyone who extends peace to us, we extend peace to them," al-Yaqoubi barked over the heads of the seated congregation. "We fight for the sake of Allah...We fight those who oppress us, who take our property and our freedom of speech...The media depict us as monsters, that we love to fight—No!"

Parts of the sermon were openly political. Al-Yaqoubi, who is considered a moderate, spoke approvingly of jihad in the battlefield, of "fighting in order to liberate your country, as the Iraqis are doing." (Asked about this afterward, he told me that it is natural to fight against an invading army. As to why Arabs so rarely rise up against their own Arab oppressors, he said it was un-Islamic to use violence against a homegrown government.)

From the pulpit, al-Yaqoubi claimed that the early Muslims who came to countries like Egypt and Syria and Iraq and North Africa did so "not to occupy land, but to liberate people who were oppressed by their governments." As for spreading Islam by force, he said, Americans should understand the concept better than anyone, since "America feels she has the right to impose democracy all over the world" and "to throw away governments that don't agree with her policy." But whereas the desire to disseminate Islam "is based on the divine," the American approach to spreading democracy "is based on greed."

Having said that, al-Yaqoubi once again took a more conciliatory approach. "This doesn't mean that we are going to practice jihad in America.

We have to show our neighbors respect. We love people around the world and want them to become Muslims."

Throughout the sermon it was as if he were playing a game—stepping as close to the edge of acceptability as possible, and then nimbly retreating. It was his good fortune that the political mood in New York was fiercely anti-Bush and anti-war, which allowed him a considerable latitude in his remarks.

Most intriguing of all, perhaps, were al-Yaqoubi's statements about the role of the Muslim immigrant in the West. While many Muslims have come here to earn money and live a better life, he said, they can justify their decision to live in a materialistic, non-Islamic country by acting as messengers for Allah. "What justifies us living in America, other than trying to convey the Message?" he asked rhetorically.

The sermon built to an impassioned, rapid-fire crescendo, in which, almost shouting, al-Yaqoubi seemed to divide jihad into foreign and domestic spheres, with appropriate action for each.

"Wherever the American troops are—wherever they are, they are going to be defeated," he yelped. But "here in this country," he instructed Muslims to "leave jihad to those who are fighting jihad," and "work peacefully" to represent Islam.

The end of the sermon signaled the time for prayer, and the atmosphere in the mosque became electric. An usher, massive and rotund as a bouncer, rushed around pushing the congregants into precise rows like Japanese commuters being squeezed into a Tokyo subway car, forcing them to stand shoulder to shoulder in line after line after line, from the back of the mosque all the way to the front. There must be no gaps that wily Satan could slip through, sowing division. As the prayers commenced, thousands of faces touched the floor with choreographed precision.

"It's a beautifully simple and elegant religion. It's extremely sensible," said Bruce ("al-Baraa") Randall, a personal trainer and student of South Asian art history from Northern California who recently converted to Islam and attends Friday prayers at the mosque. Looking at the hundreds of bent bodies, you could see what he meant.

From an observer's viewpoint, it was rather like a bizarre sartorial demonstration—look, here are the backs of a thousand jackets and the seats of a thousand trousers! Swatches of fabric in every color joined to form an immense patchwork tapestry stretching from one end of the room to the other. To a Christian, it could look strangely alluring. No hymns—no *pretending* to be singing. Even the prayers, though in Arabic, were brief and required only minimal call-and-response. Curiously, while demanding what to a Christian might appear to be like excessive uniformity and obedience, Islam seemed to permit the individual a considerable amount of personal breathing space too. And if you were a non-Arabic speaker, listening to prayers in a foreign language would, I suppose, be similar to a Catholic attending services held in Latin.

Tall and physically imposing, Randall held himself erect, radiated pride and described himself as an "independent thinker" with no intention of taking his cues from the media or following societal norms unquestioningly. Walking across the mosque's floor at the beginning of the service, he found an empty spot and sat down with a purposeful deliberation, as if that particular place had been reserved for him and him only. Yet he spoke of his own conversion with humility. Ethnically a WASP, he had been raised in an atheist household near Silicon Valley, a background that made it hard for him to take up an organized religion, even one he had grown to love. Initially, he had been drawn to Islam as an academic during a year's study in India, particularly through the medium of art history. It wasn't an issue of Islam versus some other religion, he told me, it was a question of whether he would join a large religious body or continue on his own individual path. And after a while he had conceded that his own path had run its course, that it was a dead end. He had finally concluded that "there was this religion out there that I had tremendous respect for above all others, that for me to hold onto this position that I was going to follow my own path to God was an extremely arrogant one. Do I think I know something that all those people who've followed Islam for 14 centuries don't know?"

The week before, Randall had listened to a
sermon al-Yaqoubi had given on stress-management.
Normally this would be considered an utterly
American topic, but the sheikh had managed to
make it Islamic. "He talked about the stresses
Muslims in America will feel, and he spoke about
how you could use Islam to decrease that stress,"
he told me. "I found it ironic, because I have less
stress since embracing Islam. I think I was waging
a battle for many years between the atheistic
worldview I was raised with, and my own inclinations towards religion. Those things were battling
inside me for a long time and had shut down
my heart. When I finally laid down my weapons,
I just felt much more able to breathe. It's not what
I would have predicted - I would have predicted
that I would feel *more* stress, because becoming a
Muslim runs against the grain of what you'd think
American culture would dictate for us, but my
experience has been the opposite."

In terms of religious rigor, Randall was not
yet on the level of Charles, going to the mosque
five times a day every day. He said he tried to

make a point of going to mosque once a day, sometimes here on 96th Street, at other times in Brooklyn, where he worked. He was friendly with several fellow converts, most of them recent ones like himself, and most of them Hispanic. He no longer drank alcohol, and he was newly cautious about his relationships with women.

"If it's a non-Muslim woman I'll shake her hand, but I wouldn't be alone in a room with her— that much is clear," he said. "I'm not married, and I'm more circumspect with women across the board than I used to be, particularly with Muslim women, just out of respect. My friendships with non-Muslims have continued as before, though I obviously won't go out drinking with them as I would before, but it hasn't significantly changed."

With the prayers under way, there was almost no room for the unbeliever. Two mild-mannered cameramen from India's STAR channel, who were standing next to me filming the proceedings, hurriedly folded up their tripods and disappeared. I decided to go with them. I squeezed my way to the back where the first mountain of shoes was now surrounded by more mountains, hundreds of Merrills and Nikes and Adidas and lace-ups and sandals flung down on top of each other. Outside more men were praying on the carpets provided, all in equally precise rows, and two men in wheelchairs had formed a mournful duo of their own.

Afterward, as the mosque emptied, I ran into Charles, who was shaking hands and saying *"Salaam aleikum, aleikum salaam"* to people left and right, many of whom he knew by name. He looked happy, a blissful smile of belonging on his face. Though it had put him at odds with ordinary American society, becoming a Muslim had also given him a sense of community unavailable to him when he was just another white dude into loud music, parties and girls. It had brought him distinction. The mosque was full of young Arab and South Asian men, sharply dressed businessmen with neat beards, cabdrivers in baseball caps, diminutive Bangladeshis in white robes and trousers—and religion came as naturally to them as breathing. They were entirely unselfconscious about it, and it was obvious that they considered it a source of unity and solace and power. Not for the first time I found myself wondering how it was that so many urban whites had managed to turn their own religion into an object of scorn, even a source of shame, while everyone around them continued to reap the benefits of organized faith. And, since the religious impulse showed no sign of dying out, should we be surprised if spiritually inclined urban whites decided to join a religion which, unlike Christianity, seemed to be *alive?*

"I consider that absolutely the best day of my life," he said, his face bright with happiness when I asked him about the day he took *Shahadah* three years earlier in that very mosque. "The way I describe it is, it seemed like physically and symbolically the people were emptying into me. This entire room was still full. The imam said, 'Is there anyone here who wants to take *Shahadah?*,' and my friend stood up and said, 'C'mon, c'mon.' I said, 'Now? Here? In front of everybody?' And he brought me up, and I took *Shahadah* with another guy. All I remember of that day is that no one seemed to have moved in the room. The amount of people you saw today? They still remained when I finished saying, 'I testify there is no god to be worshiped except for Allah, and Mohammed is his messenger.'"

"That's all you had to do?" I asked, just making sure.

Charles laughed. "Why, are you ready?" he replied.

THE SEARCH
FOR CONVERTS

As always, the Muslim level of confidence was striking. Converts like Charles not only lived and breathed Islam all day long, they seemed convinced that others could be persuaded to do so also. (Once, in his cab, Charles had a white American passenger who expressed interest in Islam and said he had occasionally thought about converting. Charles offered to pull over and give him *Shahadah* then and there.) The sheer *speed* with which one could officially become Muslim, complete with a new name, was stunning. Even

Heriberto Silva, the Mexican professor who through his studies had been familiar with Islam for years, seemed taken aback when the moment finally came. "I was thinking you have to take an exam, or something like that, "he told me, blinking owlishly in the center of the mosque. "But no. It was easy."

An almost comical version of this "conversion-speed" is recounted in the opening pages of Aukai Collins' 2002 memoir, *My Jihad*, in which the author describes his life as a "blue-eyed All-American mujahid holy warrior" fighting on the Muslim side in Bosnia, Chechnya, Kashmir and elsewhere during the 1990s. It all started one day in 1993, when Collins walked into a mosque (he had never been in one before) in a neighborhood of San Diego inhabited by Kurds, Pakistanis, Afghans, Somalis, and other immigrants from Muslim countries, along with black, Asian and Hispanic gangs. From his description, Collins didn't even seem to have taken *Shahadah*—in his case, he appears to have become a Muslim simply by walking into a mosque. Within hours—

moving at the pace of a character in a comic
strip—he has rented a room from a Muslim
living next door to the mosque; within weeks he
has grown "a big red beard" and adopted full
Islamic garb; and within months he has signed up
to fight for his new co-religionists in Bosnia.

Collins was suffering from an extreme
case of what Saraji Umm Zaid, over at
ModernMuslima.com, terms "Convertitis"—an ill-
ness that is highly contagious and spreads
rapidly among converts to Islam, "particularly
those who are experiencing great amounts of
confusion, but who don't think they are. (Also com-
monly known as The Case of the Insta-Scholar.)"
Symptoms include an exaggerated adherence to
Arabic-style dress and dietary codes, insistence on
being called by one's adopted Muslim name,
and talking endlessly about Islamic identity and
anti-Muslim bias and acting as if one were already
a great Koranic scholar and the sole practitioner of
"true Islam." (Charles obviously had more than a
touch of convertitis, though his symptoms were
relatively benign.)

"When you first convert, there's a real zeal toward Islam," explains Juan Alvarado, a Latino convert associated with the Alianza Islamica, a New York mosque that catered mainly to Hispanics (it had closed down recently), and with the Latino American Dawah Organization, whose online newsletter he writes for. "When I first converted I wore the *kufi*, the *jelabaya*. At work I'd wear my normal business clothing, but I'd wear my *kufi* too, and I know I must have looked like some weird eccentric! I wouldn't actually pray at the office, but I was very open with my religion. I'd tell everyone and everyone would know. But since 9/11 I've been less open about it, because some time in November that year I got a visit from someone I'm pretty sure was FBI. I don't know how he got my name and how he knew I was a Muslim, but why else would he be visiting me? In fact, he was a nice guy, he even took me out to lunch, but it was a weird visit. I felt he was trying to recruit me to be some kind of spy. He wanted to know if I could go into a group of Arabs and blend in. But I don't speak Arabic."

Following the Friday prayers, I spoke with al-Yaqoubi, who must have witnessed a few cases of convertitis in his time. (It seemed to me that he cast a wary eye on Charles.) Appearing a little tired (he had already conducted several interviews, including one for television) but at ease, he sat with me on the carpet and fingered his worry beads. He pronounced himself optimistic about Islam's prospects in the West, estimating that he gave *Shahadah* to approximately 100 Americans (of whom 20 would be white, the rest African-American, Latino and Asian) every Ramadan in New York, and had had quite a lot of success with whites in the San Francisco Bay area. The diversity of American society made it easier for Islam to take hold, he believed, because there was no dominant culture to repel it—"unless," he added with a touch of sarcasm, "you count McDonalds." In England he had had less success, but in Scandinavia there was a steady trickle of native Danes and Swedes. Overall, the picture was very positive. "If you look at statistics from the Pew Foundation, for example, about the favorability of Islam after 9/11, how it increased immediately by 13% and is still increasing, this is very encouraging," he said. "And we are witnessing this by people coming to embrace Islam."

Did he expect the number of converts to go on increasing?

"Well, it's not only my expectation actually," he replied. "Analysts like Paul Kennedy, he wrote about this in an article a few years ago in *New Perspectives Quarterly*, there was an article by him about how Islam is increasing, so I think this is expected. Work now is much better than 10 years ago, although we don't have any organized effort. Most of the people who come here come out of their own interest."

I sensed in al-Yaqoubi, as I had done in talking to el-Ashry at the mosque on 11th Street, a slight tension in the air when the subject of converts, and whether or not there might be an organized effort to convert people to Islam in America, arose. Was there a lot of that going on? I asked.

"Let me give you the following statement," al-Yaqoubi replied in smooth P.R. mode, the word

"statement" clearly suggesting a prepared response,
as if this was recognized as a danger-area. "We
don't have any organized work, missionary activities, proselytization. But some people feel guilty
living here only for the sake of money. So, they
want to find another excuse to justify their stay
in a non-Islamic land rather than their own
Islamic country. So the reason is, a good reason,
is if you're spreading the word of Islam, with
wisdom, with knowledge, calling people, then
you have an excuse to stay. But they didn't come
originally to spread the word. There's no
organized effort, missionary work, activities,
not by any organization."

It seems likely that al-Yaqoubi was being a
little disingenuous. It is true that, unlike
Christianity, Islam tends not to have professional
missionaries. But this is mainly because, as Bernard
Lewis explains in *Islam in the West*, Islam assigns the
task of *da'wa* to all Muslims alike. A significant
portion of America's Muslim community is
committed to the propagation of the faith, of
disseminating Islamic values and attaining converts

whenever possible. As one commentator wrote in the Muslim journal, *The Message*, "We have the primary task of Islamizing America. We have to carefully select our priorities, set achievable targets, and concentrate.... We have Allah's message, and a 250 million person-large target group." [8]

But specialized missionary activity exists as well. The Tableeghi Jamaat, a Muslim movement which originated in India and has a strongly anti-Western message, has been sending missionaries to the United States since 1952. The Islamic Assembly of North America is an organization formed in 1993 to pursue *da'wa* in the U.S. In 2004, it hosted a weekend-long conference in Ann Arbor, Michigan, which included a 6-hour workshop on "How to Give *Shahadah* in 10 Minutes!" [9]

Peter Leitner is a counterterrorism specialist at the Washington Center for Peace and Justice. "We track what's going on in the recruitment world around radical Islam," he told me. "Toward that end, we've seen some disturbing things. If you consider Hispanics as being white in America, Islamists have been targeting Hispanic women for marriage, particularly in Florida, California and New York.

They do this to have children who will then be future Islamists, and to try to get citizenship or a green card themselves. Some of them are involved in multi-spouse relations, having several wives. That's an area of great concern. We're talking about long-term penetration, a fifth column and all that."

Another area of concern to Leitner is al-Fuqrah, a small Islamist organization that originated in America and to which converts such as the "shoe bomber" Richard Reid, John Walker Lindh, so-called "dirty bomber" José Padilla, and the Washington sniper have all been linked. It is led by Sheikh Mubarak Ali Shah Gilani, who came to prominence as the imam of a Brooklyn mosque in the early 1980s. Gilani was shown in a recruitment video outfitted in military fatigues and ammunition belt, and he actively sought jihadists, usually among black Americans and ex-convicts. Incredibly, the sect or its members have been charged by state and Federal authorities with seventeen bombings and thirteen assassinations— mostly of Indians and even fellow imams—on

United States territory. It was Gilani himself, who had fled the U.S. for Pakistan after one of his followers was implicated in the 1993 World Trade Center bombing, that *Wall Street Journal* reporter Daniel Pearl believed he was being taken to when he was kidnapped in Karachi.

"It's a very radical Wahhabi organization run by Pakistani intelligence that has specialized over the years in recruiting African-Americans with criminal records," says Leitner. "A lot of it's taking place in prison, where they're recruiting people with a bone to pick with society to a radical form of Islam where they can continue being criminals, but now in the name of Allah. They're very clever because they set up front organizations that bid on government contracts, and they get them! So you have the phenomenon of a criminally based Wahhabi organization that works among the dispossessed and then worms its way to positions where it can get access to databases used by the police and other organizations giving access to people's credit history. They have compounds throughout the States."

Spreading Islam in America, and converting at least some Americans on the way, has also been an interest of several foreign governments and agencies, starting with the Saudis, who have made their own Wahhabi brand of Islam the dominant strain of the religion not only in America but worldwide, spending over $2.5 billion annually to maintain a global chain of Islamic institutions.[10]

In 2005, Freedom House published a disturbing 89-page report (*Saudi Publications on Hate Ideology Invade American Mosques*) that examined over 200 documents of Saudi origin found in theoretically mainstream American mosques, and concluded that they constituted a form of "hate speech." The documents, 90% of which were in Arabic, advocate murder of homosexuals, adulterers, and apostate Muslims who convert out of Islam. They encourage Muslim immigrants to despise Christians, Jews and all non-Muslim Americans in general, as well as Shi'ite and Sufi Muslims, and condemn democracy as un-Islamic. Perhaps the only encouraging thing about the report is that the documents were for the most part taken from the mosques and brought to Freedom House by Muslim Americans hostile to Wahhabism.

"It is basic to the belief of Islam that everyone who does not embrace Islam is an unbeliever and must be called an unbeliever and that they are enemies to Allah, his Prophet and the believers," reads one typically uncompromising document discovered in a San Diego mosque. Rejecting the American taste for "interfaith" dialogue, it argues that amity between religions "erases the differences between Islam and unbelief, between truth and falsehood, good and bad, and it breaks the wall of resentment between Muslims and nonbelievers, so that there is no loyalty and enmity, no more jihad and fighting to raise Allah's word on earth." [11]

Any convert to Islam is likely to run into some form of Wahhabism in American mosques. "They themselves don't call themselves Wahhabis, they consider themselves part of the whole Sunni tradition, just a more austere version created in Saudi Arabia," says Alvarado. "Have I met people like that? I've met people in Islam that I feel a resentment [towards], because it's as though they expect you to be a walking Islamic encyclopedia and know-it-all. If I make a mistake, correct me, but don't talk to me as if you were my father."

Alvarado tries to maintain a balance between adhering to the tenets of Islam himself and not being overly harsh on those who wander from the path. If he sees Muslims drinking alcohol, or eating during Ramadan, he'll "give them a face, kind of a stare down," but he won't criticize them verbally. On the other hand, he won't associate with them either. "To live Islam, I guess it's an austere religion when you compare it to normal people in daily life. Not to say that Muslims aren't normal, but I was born a Christian, a Catholic, and they don't pray five times a day. So when they see you doing it, it's deep for them! I pray five times a day and sometimes more. For someone looking from the outside in, maybe it's too crazy, too strict. But from the inside it doesn't feel that way."

While it was easy to be captivated by Muslim self-confidence and the vision of more and more Americans and Europeans, accustomed to secularism or diluted versions of Christianity, bowing down to Allah, Islam remains a pretty tough sell in the West, particularly among whites.

Agha Jaffri, a leader of the Shi'a community in New York, believes that the number of whites converting is extremely small. "The people at CAIR [Council of American-Islamic Relations] will exaggerate the daylight out of you that every other person is becoming a Muslim, but that's garbage," he said. "They do have great deal of gains in prison system with blacks and Hispanics, but it's not significant with whites. The Salafis and Wahhabis lie like hell. They have this trip to aggrandizement. If converts are around, they're going to Sufism, which is anathema to fundamentalist Muslims. They hate Sufis. I can see that happening, but even there I don't see a deluge."

Stephen Schwartz, the author of *The Two Faces of Islam* and a former religion correspondent for the *San Francisco Chronicle*, is also doubtful about Islam's attractiveness to Westerners. Now 66, he himself converted at the age of 49 following what he calls "a long intellectual and then emotional process" born of his longstanding interest in Sufism and the Islamic heritage in Spain and the Balkans. A sharp critic of Wahhabism, he places his own

Muslim faith in the more liberal, multicultural tradition of Balkan Islam. But he doesn't see many whites following in his footsteps.

"I don't think it's a deepening trend or that it's going to appeal to a large number of people," he said. "It's always been a marginal trend and it's not going to stop being a marginal trend. First of all, it's not an easy religion to engage with in the way some others are. For instance, a person who's going to become a Muslim in the West is probably someone who's done a lot of drinking in their lives. If your lifestyle is that of an ordinary Westerner, male or female, and are used to drinking a lot of wine or beer, that's not going to be easy, and most other religions aren't going to ask you to do that. That's a pretty substantial change to make.

"Above all it requires spiritual discipline, seriousness, unless you're going to become a faddist bonehead Wahhabi," he said, citing some of the immediate dilemmas that confront a potential convert, the first being whether to choose Sunni Islam (three-quarters of the world's Muslim's are Sunni) or Shi'a Islam, which is followed by Iran and most of southern Iraq. There are also four main schools of Islamic law— *Malaki, Shafi, Hanafi,* and *Hanbali*—which should the convert affiliate himself with? "You kind of have to defend it, it's what you have to do if you expect to have a voice in the community," said Schwartz. "It's pretty demanding. There will be John Walker Lindh types, or other converts like these French extremists who are looking for the negation of Western culture, but that's not going to grow. I think that Sufism in the West may grow marginally, but it will remain minor compared to Buddhism."

ANXIOUS EUROPE

Whether or not Islam is catching on among native Western populations, there is no doubt that the conversion phenomenon is being watched carefully. Because of its falling birth rate, burgeoning Muslim population and fading attachment to its Judeo-Christian religious inheritance, Europe is felt to be especially vulnerable to Islam. At the end of World War II there were less than one million Muslims living in Europe. Now there are an estimated 20 million, with five to six million in France, three million in Germany, two million in

Britain, one million in both Italy and Holland, and 500,000 in both Austria and Spain. Mosques are plentiful: France and Germany have five or six thousand apiece, and most other European countries have at least a thousand.[12]

"In Europe in particular you will find so many mosques are being built in what used to be churches," says Mateen Siddiqui of the ISCA. "The Muslims will come and say, 'This church is empty and no one is attending,' and the people in charge will say they're trying to sell it, and they will buy it for a very low price and make it into a mosque." Europeans may not actually want to go to church themselves, but that doesn't mean they want to see their houses of worship disappear or, worse, be replaced by those of a rival faith openly dedicated to global religious supremacy. One can trace the anxiety merely by scanning the headlines about the growth of Islam: "Decline and Fall of the Christian Empire." "Is Europe the New 'Dark Continent'?" "Faith: Islam's Third Run for Europe." "The Triumph of the East." "Bowing to Islam." "No Wonder Our Kids Are Turning to Islam." "Europe Fears Converts May Aid Extremism."

"Muslim France." "Growing Number of Germans
Embracing Islam." "The Coming of Eurabia."

Then there is the spectre of terrorism. Radicalized white recruits are of obvious value to al-Qaeda, since they foil any attempt at ethnic profiling. France's anti-terrorism chief, Jean-Louis Bruguière, believes converts make for the toughest and most fanatical terrorists, with France providing an increasing number of them, including women.[13] Leitner mentions Bosnians "who are blond, blue eyed and look like Swedes, and who are some of the most radicalized and trained [Islamists] in the world." But he concedes that it's often hard to tell to what extent the attempt to convert people is programmatic and driven by politics or simply the by-product of an inherently proselytizing religion.

The Spanish judge, Baltasar Garzon, who recently presided over the sentencing of Yusuf Galan, a Spanish convert accused of aiding the 9/11 plotters, seems less concerned with whether or not someone has formally become a Muslim. "I don't think it matters whether they are or are not converts," he told me through a translator after a conference on terrorism at New York University.

Though Galan has been given a ten-year prison sentence for playing a peripheral role in the 9/11 attacks, Garzon noted that there were also non-converts sympathetic to the Islamist cause who cooperated in the terrorist attack on the Madrid train station on March 11, 2004. In other words, if you can't find an actual convert, a fellow traveler may do.

All kinds of claims are made; some sound like material for a first-rate cinematic thriller. For instance, the widely read Israeli-based web site, *Debka File*, paints a compelling picture of jihadist infiltration of the glossy new Europe of Starbucks and the youthful ipod-wearing laptop brigade, with outwardly secular, westernized Muslim secret agents perpetually on the prowl for disaffected whites who might be persuaded to conspire against their own societies in service of Islamic revolution. The tone of the prose is breathless and seductive; reading it, any fan of espionage fiction could hardly fail to be enthralled:

> Recruitment across Europe continues apace
> and in greater secrecy than ever as a result of a

switch to new recruiting techniques and appeal
to fresh target-populations for building the
Euro army.... Al Qaeda, intent on beating
surveillance and penetration by intelligence
services, no longer selects combatants at its
usual hunting grounds in mosques, Islamic
culture centers and Muslim immigrant
neighborhoods. Instead, native Europeans
freshly converted to Islam are targeted.

The new campaign is styled "the white
recruitment drive" or "coffee shop conscription."
Operational cells and recruiting agents patronize
ordinary cafes on the high streets of Europe's
major cities where they blend into the crowds.
The new conscripts defy identification by
European intelligence services because their
Islamic lives are lived completely underground.
There is therefore no way of finding their
addresses [and] telephone numbers. Unit-level
meetings or training session, attended by 30 or
40 men, may take place under cover of social
activity such as a holiday camp in a remote
part of Europe. Tracking them down is getting

harder as bin Laden's new Euro army expands at the rate of tens of thousands and when "white" recruits may already form some 25 percent of the total.[14]

As the French scholar Olivier Roy has remarked, following the death of Marxism only two internationalist movements remain available to the young Western rebel: the anti-globalization movement and radical Islam, both of which are also pillars of anti-Americanism. The only problem for the would-be political rebel contemplating conversion to Islam, a skeptic might argue, is Islam itself. After all, its radically restrictive treatment of women makes it unlikely that many females will apply (though Michelle Leslie, an Australian underwear model, is said to have converted to Islam after being jailed on drug charges in Bali, and reemerged in a burqa), while for the males, a life of constant prayer, fasting, abstention from alcohol and women, etc., is hardly the stuff of which secret-agent fantasies are made.

Nor are the convert-terrorists always James Bond material themselves. Stephen Paul Paster, a member of al-Fuqrah, blew his hand off while planting a bomb in Portland, Oregon in 1983. Ironically, he now provides explosives training to aspiring bombers in Lahore, Pakistan. Then there's Jack Roche, the burly Australian factory worker who converted to Islam in order to overcome an alcohol problem. Dubbed "the naïve militant" by the BBC, he was invited to Afghanistan in 1999, only to find himself sitting across a table from Osama bin Laden. "Whoa, that's like the bloke on the telly," Roche reportedly told himself, having had no idea that he was going to be lunching with one of the world's most wanted men.

The 50-year-old Roche had hoped to sign on with the Taliban, whose struggle he felt it was his duty as a good Muslim to join. Instead, he was given the usual explosives training and sent back to Australia, where he was instructed to conduct video surveillance of the Israeli Embassy in Canberra, on which an attack was being planned.

(It was eventually abandoned.) Posing as an architecture buff with an odd fascination for buildings containing a large number of Israelis, he even got into a conversation with an embassy security guard, who, noticing the amount of filming he was doing, joked that he probably intended "to bomb the joint." The enormity of what he was involved in gradually dawned on Roche, who turned himself in first to the American Consulate and then to the Australian Security Intelligence Organization. Neither the Americans nor the Australians seemed terribly interested in this improbable terrorist, and it was only after the Bali bombings of 2002 that he was finally arrested and sentenced to nine years' imprisonment.[15]

Since people convert to different religions all the time, in theory there should be nothing note-worthy in itself about a Westerner converting to Islam as opposed to, say, becoming a Hari Krishna or Moonie or Mormon or Buddhist or Branch Davidian or anything else. Unfortunately, due to its all-encompassing nature, lack of church/state separation and the myriad political tensions that surround it, contemporary Islam seems to create a

unique set of difficulties as it intersects with the
more liberal lifestyle of the West.

Recently I spoke with a European businessman
who had experienced some of these problems
directly. He had lived in America during the
1980s. At the end of that decade, he had returned
to Europe, and fallen in love with a French woman
with whom he lived for a certain amount of time.
They had a daughter together but did not marry,
and then later separated. Now he was back in
New York, while the mother of his child, who is
still in Europe, had married a North African
immigrant, a "fundamentalist" according to the
businessman, and converted to Islam. The last
time he had seen her she was wearing the *hijab* and
a skirt that ended at her ankles.

That bothered him, certainly, but what worried
him—gnawed at him, even—was the fact that his
daughter, now ten, was being brought up in a
Muslim household. For the time being, she was
still being raised as a Catholic, but with a convert
mother and a Muslim step-father, not to mention

a new addition to the household—a younger half-sister who was definitely being raised as a Muslim—she was in a distinct minority. She was too young to wear the *hijab*, but once she reached puberty, the businessman feared this would be her fate, and that, like some other Muslim female students in Europe, she could end up going through school without being allowed to study biology or partake in sports, and might even be removed by her step-father from the classroom altogether.

"The schism is more in the fact that there are two parents from different religions and lifestyles," he told me. "It may not seem much, but it creates in a person's mind a void, a lack of belonging anywhere. The real drama exists in my daughter's mind, and what her life will be in the future. She's going to have to make a choice.

"There is nothing wrong with the religious aspect of Islam, it's a way of life," he added in a more conciliatory tone at odds with his body language, which suggested barely suppressed rage. "What is being put into question is the role of a woman in society. The relationship the woman has to men—these are the radical changes. These are the things that clash. The biology class, all of that, that's just details. The broader picture is how this daughter now lives, without a sense of her place as a woman in society. She's in a situation where the woman is subservient to the man—in her own household. And all this in the middle of western Europe! For me this is a clear example of the clash of civilizations. How it has entered the family nucleus, and how the war has entered the home.

"I'm not the only guy this has happened to," he concluded grimly. "There are a lot of others." In the end, he predicted, civil war would break out in Europe, and he would go back to fight.

"The fact that increasing numbers of young Germans want to join an alien and hostile ghetto within the country of their birth is unsurprising," wrote the controversial Serbian journalist and harsh critic of Islam, Srdja Trifkovic, in 2003. "Estranged from their parents, ignorant of their culture, ashamed of their history, those young converts are making a logical step on the path of alienation that alternatively leads to madness, drugs or suicide. They accurately sense that 'those who subscribe to Islam and its civilization are aliens, regardless of their clothes, their professions or their places of residence,'" Trifkovic wrote, quoting commentator Sam Francis, "and they choose to be aliens.... Tackling the meaning of Incarnation, Trinity or Fall is not even an option when a readily available alternative offers simplicity and instant gratification. It is as easy to say, 'Allah is great; there is no Allah but Allah, and Muhammad is His prophet,' as it is to gulp a gram of Ecstasy."

Given that Trifkovic was reacting to a 2003 newspaper article estimating the number of native Germans to have converted to Islam at a mere 12,400, it could be argued that his reaction was overwrought. On the other hand, it's hard to imagine any impartial reader of the 2004 French government investigation, led by Jean-Pierre Obin, the inspector general of French education, on the rabid Islamization of many French schools, not being alarmed. In areas of urban France with a large North African Muslim population, Obin's report states, local schools have fallen victim to a pathological strain of fundamentalist Islam which not only affects Muslim students, but non-Muslim ones as well. Trifkovic may have compared the act of *Shahadah* to swallowing a gram of Ecstasy, but for some kids it's more like taking a dose of cod liver oil.

The zealotry Obin describes in his 37-page report is extraordinary—students refusing to share a swimming pool with women or unbelievers and insisting on separate "halal" eating and bathing areas; the outright rejection on religious grounds of French literary giants such as Flaubert, Rousseau, and Voltaire; the enforcement of draconian dress codes on female Muslim students; challenging the validity of all non-Muslim calendar holidays such as Christmas and Easter; the refusal to use any mathematical symbol that even vaguely resembles a cross, etc. For young women the situation is often so bad that a protest group, Ni Putes, Ni Soumises ("Neither Whores, Nor Submissives"), has sprung up to defend the rights of women in Muslim ghettoes, arguing for the separation of church and state as fundamental to female liberty. During Ramadan, in particular, the tremendous pressure exerted by students on other students to behave in super-orthodox fashion means that many non-Muslims, forced into conforming with the majority, end up fasting during the month as well. Given all this, it's no surprise to learn in the report that a considerable number of non-Muslim students, bowing to peer pressure and the drumbeat of constant proselytization, finally convert to Islam themselves.[16]

Islam's reluctance to compromise is not always a negative; there are some positive aspects as well. "One of the richnesses of Islam," writes Timothy J. Winter, a 45-year-old British convert and lecturer in Islamic Studies at Cambridge University now known as Sheikh Abdul Hakim Murad, "is that the core liturgy, the core practices of worshiping and of fasting and of charity, are the same everywhere and have never changed. No well-meaning, liberal, woolly-minded reformers have said, 'Let's do mosque worship in a slightly different way. Let's bring in the guitars and the trendy imam'. I go into a mosque and I know exactly what I'm going to get, a beautiful, unchanged, perfect ritual from a great

age of faith, and I find that to be a unique privilege, one of the great things of being a Muslim."

Even Michel Houellebecq, the prescient French novelist who was taken to court in Paris by a coalition of Muslim and human rights groups for inciting anti-Muslim hatred after he called Islam the world's "stupidest" religion in an interview (he was acquitted), acknowledges that there are beneficial aspects to the conversion phenomenon. Though an atheist himself, he told me that unlike many of his literary peers he has never underestimated religion's ability to ease the burdens of life and the need many people feel for it. Ironically, Houellebecq believes it is harder for a secular French person to reignite internally the moribund Catholic faith of his forefathers than it is to take up an entirely new one. Thus Islam—new, exacting, alien—becomes an increasingly intriguing alternative.

Houellebecq also suggested that sexually insecure young men may convert in the belief that if they marry a Muslim woman she will at least be faithful, whereas in the secular erotic jungle fidelity remains very much in doubt. Furthermore, for members of the white underclass, Islam delivers a strict moral code that can help lift them out of drug addiction, alcoholism, petty crime, and the like. In France, Catholicism no longer seems to have the power to do so.

Could Houellebecq imagine a future in which large numbers of French people converted? I asked.

"Oh yes, it's easy to imagine, because there is nothing that can prevent it," he responded in his fractured English. "It's free in terms of religion—like America. I think a religion can appear and develop today, it's possible. You can see easily when you go in certain places that there are more and more veiled women, with more and more covering. It [hasn't come] to the point where bin Laden would be a true hero for these people. I think that most of them would admit that bin Laden goes too far! It could become more dramatic—maybe it will be. It's hard to predict. It's very hard to predict in general the Muslims. If someone says he can predict the future of any sociological phenomenon, I think he lies."

In Europe, some say the withdrawal of traditional Western religious instruction from the public arena has allowed Islam to step into the moral breach. Muslims often speak of the West as a materialistic wasteland of drug addiction, teen pregnancies, depression, pornography and loss of community. The imam of the 96th Street mosque, Omar Abu Namous, offers the traditional rigors of Islam (stop drinking, stop fornicating, pray five times a day and fast during Ramadan) as an alternative to an increasingly "lax" Christianity that demands little of its adherents beyond occasional church attendance and a vague loyalty to the precepts of love, charity and compassion.

Of course, it is not only Muslims who rail at Western decadence. In Birmingham, England, a city with a sizable Muslim presence (its largest mosque was until recently named after Saddam Hussein), I spent a couple of days with Theodore Dalrymple, the conservative journalist, just before he retired as a slum doctor and prison psychiatrist. A perceptive critic of militant Islam, Dalrymple has nonetheless often found himself feeling strangely sympathetic to the plight of traditionalist Muslim parents who don't want their British-born sons and daughters to embrace the local know-nothing "yob" culture. He gave me a tour of Birmingham's festive main drag on a Saturday night, and the packed thoroughfare was a non-stop carnival of booze and drugs and fast food and night clubs, with an undercurrent of potential violence and young men vomiting and young girls collapsing dead drunk on the street. And yet, much as he despises Birmingham's popular culture, Dalrymple is horrified by the virtual imprisonment in their homes of Muslim girls who will often be shipped back to Pakistan for arranged marriages they look on with dread. For Dalrymple, it's a tragedy of Shakespearian proportions.

He quotes Juliet's imploring speech in *Romeo and Juliet*: "Is there no pity sitting in the clouds that sees into the depths of my despair? O sweet my mother, cast me not away, delay this marriage." Incredible as it may seem, he says, Shakespeare's words accurately express the plight of many Muslim girls in 21st century Birmingham. "Because if they don't get married to the man their father wants them to, they can even be killed." But

even here he is torn, since it is his opinion, based on close professional observation, that Muslim girls forcibly removed from British schools at the age of 12 due to their parents' fear of cultural contamination are actually much better educated, in a broad sense, than the white "sluts" (as he terms them) who attend school for another five years.

"And furthermore, when you speak to the Muslim girls, they are people of high caliber. They are well mannered, decent people. So in other words, their upbringing, though it's led to this terrible denouement if you like, is nevertheless superior to the way the white girls are brought up. There's no question they're vastly superior in intelligence, in manners, in outlook, to the white girls. And one of the problems with the kind of scene that you saw last night, is that the Muslim fathers would see that and say, 'Well, I don't want our children to grow up like that.' And I can't really blame them. Can you blame them? So then they become even more conservative and entrenched."

Being outsiders, Muslims are often permitted to adopt strict moral positions which would be frowned upon in other religious commentators, particularly Christian ones. As a high-profile Muslim convert, this is an advantage that the afore-mentioned Cambridge convert Winter, has availed himself of. In his writings, he not only openly criticizes homosexuality and female immodesty, but also advocates single-sex schooling and suggests that it would be preferable if male business executives were prevented from having female secretaries, since a woman's presence in the office is likely to provoke extramarital entanglements.

Nonetheless, in an essay entitled "The Fall of the Family," Winter makes an interesting point, one that is rarely touched upon. The mores of many Muslim immigrants may be out of step with those of the average secular European or American, but they would not have been considered nearly so retrograde by secular Americans and Europeans of the 1950s and pre-Beatles-era 1960s. Study a photograph of a New York street scene in 1955 or even 1963 and you will see men dressed conservatively in suits and women in dresses that would not be considered excessively immodest by most Muslims today. "The family lifestyle of the average Syrian or Turk is not that of a modern European," writes Winters. "His clothes, furnishing, marriage rituals, and most details of life are more redolent of the 1940s and 1950s than that of the present realities of Western existence." Which, according to Winters, leaves the Muslim newcomers as "the sole defenders of values which would be recognized as legitimate by earlier generations of Britons."[17]

It's hard to know what to make of this assertion, since it is both true and untrue, or perhaps more about nostalgia than genuine attraction. Yes, many Muslims defend traditional values, but the younger generation in particular is often grotesquely anti-Western, wildly hypocritical and filled with hatred and anti-Semitism. And not only the younger generation. Abu Namous attained his present position as the imam of the mosque on 96th Street only after his predecessor, Sheikh Muhammad Gemeaha, fled New York two weeks after 9/11. Back in his native Egypt,

Gemeaha promptly informed the Arab media that Muslim children were being poisoned by Jewish doctors in American hospitals and that Zionists had masterminded the plot against the World Trade Center.

Pace Winter, it might be truer to say that few religious communities in the urban West uphold traditional values the way Muslims do. Moreover, Muslim leaders make it quite clear, unlike most of their Christian and Jewish peers, that they are willing to fight for those values and not give in to secular browbeating. In New York, for instance, it has been noted that the mosques have rebuffed all attempts at outreach by the gay community, in effect refusing to have anything to do with it, in marked contrast to most of their Christian and Jewish counterparts. One militant group, named Islamic Thinkers, which includes white converts and preaches jihad in Times Square and Jackson Heights, Queens, openly vilifies gays and has even physically attacked them, just as their similarly belligerent counterparts have done in European countries such as Holland. In their careful study of the West, Muslim leaders have no doubt also

perceieved that once the secularization of religion
begins, it has no end.

"Christians were once the same like us, and
Jews," Namous told me during a kind of informal
press conference at the end of a prayer service at
the 96th Street mosque. "But the culture of our
present times has diluted religion. It's not the
original concentration. The Europeans were very
clever in taking people away from religion. For
example, they started making jokes about clergymen,
calling them 'wet blankets' to minimize their
importance and to call them hypocrites, self-right-
eous. So people lost their faith in them."

Namous laughed heartily at all this, displaying
a set of jutting lower teeth. He seemed particularly
tickled by the phrase "wet blankets," which he
may have picked up from a British diplomat while
serving in his previous post at the UN, or perhaps
even from his readings in the English novel.
Nonetheless, it was obvious that he had no intention of allowing the same mistake to occur in the
case of Islam. Recently he had been invited to

speak during a Sunday church service downtown, and found only twenty people scattered among the pews. It wasn't something he wanted to see happen in his own house of worship, where not only did he sermonize to thousands of people, he was surrounded by eager reporters afterwards as well.

This was especially true on the day I met him. The New York City transit authority was on high alert due to what later proved to be a fraudulent tip that Islamist terrorists were about to blow up several subway stations. Yet rather than encouraging congregants to cooperate with the authorities, outside the mosque a sharply dressed representative from CAIR distributed leaflets advising them to refer any inquiries from the FBI to their attorneys or to CAIR. ("If they come to your home, do not open the door, unless they have a warrant. You can ask them to leave their card outside your door.")

Ironically, inside the mosque Abu Namous was getting a bit of a grilling himself. As a crowd of other journalists and a group of poker-faced "interfaith" guests stood around and watched, two female Indian reporters were quietly but persistently asking nettlesome questions. Why was contemporary Islam so militant? Why did it demand the subservience of women? Why did the Taliban blow up the statues of the Buddha? Why do Muslims respond to an ever-increasing array of perceived grievances through grossly violent means? Despite their obduracy, they received no satisfaction. Their questions were crudely deflected and they were treated instead to mini-lectures on the glories of *al-Andalus*, the horrors of the Christian Inquisition, and even—a bold move on Namous' part given the reporters' obvious belief in male-female equality—the virtues of polygamy. Had the Germans permitted the practice after their defeat in World War II, he speculated, far fewer German widows would have been forced to prostitute themselves in order to make ends meet, since they would at least have had a (shared) husband to protect them financially. An interesting theory, certainly, but a strange one to be listening to on the Upper East Side.

"Islam now is a Western religion," stated Olivier Roy in 2004 at what was billed as the "Woodstock" of terrorism conferences sponsored by New York University's Center on Law and Security. "We have Muslims in Western Europe. We have Muslims in America. They are citizens. Their children will be citizens. So it is a fact."

Yes, but for all that, it didn't *sound* like a very Western religion as it emerged during Namous' mini-press conference on the Upper East Side of Manhattan. Most of all, it was profoundly un-Western in its refusal to entertain even the slightest criticism of itself or of its history. Precisely for that reason, perhaps, it contained an unmistakable potency. "Man cannot live without religion. Man is too *weak* to live without religion," Abu Namous warned, raising his index finger in the air for emphasis. Yet his voice sounded gentle. "This universe belongs to God. We are here like guests. It doesn't belong to us. Whatever you have, one day you are going to die and leave everything. It's not yours. So everything is on loan. Your life on loan, your children on loan, your money on loan, everything is on loan here. And you have to dispose of whatever you have in the way prescribed by God."

For a moment, lulled by his words and the

cadences of his sentences, I was reminded of Ka, the poet-atheist-hero of Orhan Pamuk's novel, *Snow*, who, after a long period of weary exile in secular Germany, returns to a provincial corner of Turkey and immediately falls under the magnetic sway of a revivified Islam. Pamuk describes the war between Ka's head and heart as he listens to the soothing words of a "reactionary sheikh":

> Something was happening that I had secretly dreaded for a long time and that in my atheist years I would have denounced as weakness and backwardness: I was returning to Islam…. A feeling of peace spread through me; I had not felt this way for years. I immediately understood that I could talk to him about anything, tell him all about my life, and he would bring me back to the path that I had always believed in, deep down inside, even as an atheist: the road to God Almighty. I was joyous at the mere expectation of this salvation.

"Are you ever afraid," I asked Abu Namous, "that Islam itself will become diluted by its exposure to the West?"

Namous said he was not, and emphasized his lack of fear by tapping authoritatively on the cover of his leather-bound Koran, which he then opened to display its glittering, gilt-edged pages.

"Some Muslims can be absorbed by Western culture, yes, but there will still be a core of Muslims who will stay faithful and loyal to this book, all the time. And this was prophesied by the Prophet Muhammad. We have a deep sense that this is the only book in the world that includes the literal and true word of God. The *only* book! So if you want to have access to the word of God, you come to *this* book. You don't go to any other book."

ISLAM LITE

"Islam is in its origins an Arab religion," writes V. S. Naipaul in the prologue to *Beyond Belief: Islamic Excursions Among the Converted Peoples*. "Everyone not an Arab who is a Muslim is a convert. Islam is not simply a matter of conscience or private belief. It makes imperial demands. A convert's worldview alters. His holy places are in Arab lands; his sacred language is Arabic. His idea of history alters. He rejects his own; he becomes, whether he likes it or not, a part of the Arab story."

If any mosque could contradict Naipaul's words, it would surely be the Masjid al-Farah (The Mosque of Divine Ease) in New York's Tribeca district, housed between the Tribeca Tavern ("Food till 3 AM!") and The Cercle Rouge, another fashionable restaurant with (on the night I was there) a snazzy looking orange motor bike parked outside. On Thursday evenings the mosque doubles as a *durga*, a Sufi house of worship where the congregation is richly multicultural and the resident sheikh is a sheikha—a white, female sheikh. This, one might say, is Islam Lite, or Islam White, and many mainstream Muslims would say it is not Islam at all. (It was easy to imagine the look of utter disgust that would appear on Charles' face were he to witness the goings-on *chez* the Mosque of Divine Ease.) In fact, seeing three of the youthful white worshippers standing outside—a young, model-handsome blonde man in a striped blue-and-white shirt talking to two equally attractive white Sufi women, lavishly wrapped about in diaphanous scarves, was like looking at some future *Vanity Fair* photo-spread on an outbreak of "cool" Islam downtown.

I asked one of the women, Juliet (her Islamic name was Rabia), a dark-haired beauty dressed in flowing blues and whites, whether she considered herself a Muslim. "That's a really hard question because there are a lot of parts of Islam that bother me," she replied, alluding in particular to its segregation of women. Instead, she referred to herself as a "dervish." And would she be attending the Friday prayers at this same mosque the following day? It seemed not. "It's a really different crowd," she responded. "You'll see if you go."

Kristine, a self-confident, well-educated woman who hailed from Colorado and had lived extensively in London, mentioned that whenever she got into a cab in New York and said "*Salaam Aleikum*" to the invariably Muslim driver, she'd get a very surprised look in response. (And no wonder—despite her expensive-looking sheer black-and-gold *hijab*, she was unmistakably an infidel Westerner.) But she refused to talk on the record unless I was granted permission to interview her by Sheikha Fariha al-Jerrahi. Unfortunately, the sheikha (*née* Philippa Fredreich), a former Roman Catholic from Houston, Texas, informed me through the organization's secretary that she would not even consent to being interviewed herself. (This came as a surprise. Though I knew it would be difficult to talk to women who had converted to a strict form of Islam, I had expected the Sufis to be far more open.)

Although it is banned outright in Saudi Arabia and Iran, and frowned upon in countries such as Syria and Jordan and Egypt, Sufism is the gateway to Islam for many American converts. There are Sufi circles all over the country, and they tend to attract an affluent, educated crowd—spiritual seekers with Ph.D's who see Sufism as an extension of their interest in the arts and desire for a more tolerant, relaxed form of spirituality. Through Sufism, some converts will graduate to the more orthodox ways of Islam found in the mosques. Others, repelled by the least sniff of compulsion or politicization, will retreat to the safety of their chanting circles and never fully identify as Muslims in the conventional sense.

"The U.S. is probably the best place where we can practice as we like," I was told by Farhad Ameli, an Iranian-born Sufi who attends a Sufi circle in Pasadena, California. "When people come to our group they see a multicultural gathering worshiping the same God, and there is no distinction whether you were born Muslim or a convert. I go to mosque regularly, and I see one convert, a white person who goes there, and that's it. But in our Sufi circle you have maybe about two dozen people, and most are American converts—white, Spanish. I think the attraction with white people is to Sufism in general."

Usually, Thursday evenings at the Tribeca mosque start off quietly enough with an informal talk given by the sheikha, seated on the carpet, with her followers seated likewise around her. She speaks about being present with Allah and about remaining focused, even when we are worn down by the daily grind. The Prophet Muhammad never lost his focus she tells the assembly. Even when he was on his long night journey to Jerusalem, "his heart never swerved." We should practice aware-ness, practice stillness of the heart and not being pulled by the powerful magnet of Creation. "If we focus in the heart, we can't get worn down, we will be in touch with the center of our own heart, which is continually overflowing with Allah's grace," she concludes.

But this is far from a sermon, with the sheikha often asking questions of her listeners and publicly welcoming newcomers.

"What's your name?" she inquires of a young man seated a short distance away.

"Jed," he replies.

"Jed," she repeats, mulling the name over. "Is that short for something?"

"Uh, no."

"Right."

The talk and chit-chat over, the sheikha opens the prayer book ("The Exalted Litany of the great Pir Nureddin Jerrahi, May his holy secret be triumphant," reads the inscription on the title page), to begin a series of chants and prayers. One entreaty, enunciated in Arabic by all assembled—*Astaghfiru-Llah* ("Forgive us, Allah!")—is repeated no less than 100 times, though I have the feeling that the sheikha is able to keep only an approximate count. Still, it looks exhausting. Other phrases—*Wa'ghfir lana bi-Fadlika Ya Rahmanu Ya Rahim* ("Forgive us

through your Grace, O Most Compassionate,
O Most Merciful") are reiterated only a handful of
times. The aim, it seems, is slowly to induce a kind
of trance mentality.

It was "George," the professor of business
management I first encountered studying Arabic
with Omar Pacheco at the 96th Street mosque,
who originally told me about the Sufi Circle at the
Masjid al-Farah. A trim, mild-looking Vietnam
veteran just shy of 60, he could easily have passed
for someone 10 years younger. Perhaps his religious
practice had something to do with it, for he seemed
uncommonly contented and serene. If *Shari'a*, or
Islamic law, is what Muslims think of as the
"external" route to God, Sufism offers the *tariqa*, or
the path, which emphasizes inner spirituality.

"Ecstasy is considered an important element to
the Sufi, both in prayer and practice, and that's the
part that's tricky, because sobriety is often seen as
a key element of Islam," he said. "Sobriety is part
of the Sufi path too, but it's a sobriety about how
screwed up the world is, and about not losing
oneself in the illusions of this world—*that's* the
sobriety. I think there's a lot of freedom in the Sufi

path. I love to do the prayers and practices of Islam, but there are times when it could be oppressive if there was no ecstasy in it."

George's original Sufi teacher, Pir Vilayat Inayat Khan, had "a very special quality of being able to read someone's soul, and see what their inclinations were, and to lead them toward those inclinations," he told me. What Pir Vilayat saw in George was a love for the Sufi tradition, for the ritual of prayers and a reverence for the Prophet Muhammad, and he saw it long before George himself became aware of it. (Vilayat, whose father had founded the Sufi Order in London in 1916, was no ordinary teacher.) Following his stint in Vietnam, George studied for a Ph.D in business but decided to "drop out" without completing it. In 1975 he moved to Canada to start an organic farm, planning to live off the land for the rest of his life. Some time after that he moved south of the border again, and joined a Sufi community in upstate New York. He stayed for seven years, studying with Pir Vilayat. ("Pir," meaning "elder, wise one," is a special rank of Sufi.)

"In India, gurus would sit with someone and give them information—*darshan* (blessing)— and my teacher would give *darshan*, and sat with me. I'd been there seven years, worked at the community bakery, figured I was doing everything I needed to do to be a spiritual person. Pir Vilayat sat with me and said, 'You know, you're not fulfilling your soul.' He didn't know anything about my past, or that I'd studied business. He said, 'There are people in the business world who need to know about Sufism.' It was a real shock to me. I'd done my doctorate, except for my dissertation, and dropped out almost ten years earlier, and on his advice I went back and completed it at Syracuse University. That was a very valuable thing for me. My life has been totally changed by that moment with him!"

Though he was reluctant fully to identify himself as a Muslim, in part because his Sufi teachings encouraged him to learn from all religions, George said he tried to pray at a mosque at least two or three times a week. Which mosque he prayed in depended on where he was on any given day, but he estimated he had worshiped in 10-15 different New York mosques overall. As often as not, whether he was worshiping in Manhattan, Long Island or Queens, he was the only white American in the congregation.

"It doesn't really bother me any more, to be honest," replied this genial man who admitted that he was probably often mistaken for an FBI agent, when asked what it was like to be in such a tiny minority. "Most practitioners at a mosque don't pay any attention to where people are from. Occasionally I see one or two WASP types, but I don't think there are many. The most important thing is my relation with God, it's one to one. And sometimes being in a mosque, part of the purpose of that is sharing that realization with others."

I read him Naipaul's quote about converts. Was there any truth to that? "No, not at all, not for me," he replied. "I don't discount any of my roots that are connected to Christianity, Buddhism, etc. That's a very narrow perspective."

From back-to-nature to behind the wheel of an SUV, George is in some ways a typical '60s character. But not many ex-dropouts, let

alone white American professors of business
management, have gone on the *haj*, as he did
five years ago when he undertook the religious
pilgrimage to Saudi Arabia.

"I never had one moment of feeling that I wasn't
part of that community," George said of his time
in Mecca. "It was totally welcoming. Of course
the Saudi guards are unwelcoming to *everybody*,
but everyone else was very friendly. I'd be sitting
there in meditation, and I'd open my eyes and
there'd be a meal in front of me. Someone would
have just left it there as a gift. Mecca is a protected
zone, so you can't go unless you're on a pilgrimage.
It's very interesting because it's the most liberated
Islam you'll find anywhere in the world. It's the
only mosque in the Muslim world where men and
women pray side by side, because everyone is in a
circle there rather than in rows. It's just a very
beautiful place, with a very strong current of
spiritual energy."

But what would the Saudis make of George's
Sufi shenanigans at the mosque in Tribeca, where,
as the evening wears on, worshippers link hands,

dance, and to the tune of *oud* and drum, chant *illahis*, mystical hymns of the Jerrahi order of dervishes:

> *Since my heart became lost in you*
> *Every cell is longing for you.*
> *Since my mind became lost in you*
> *Every thought is longing for you.*

On the sidewalk outside, where one or two Sufis will occasionally repair for a cigarette break, it's a typical late summer evening in one of the trendier neighborhoods of lower Manhattan. Two doors down, outside a bar-restaurant called Another Room, a mixed group of twenty-somethings drink cocktails and pints of beer while, in front of them, a young woman stands in high heels, glancing at her watch and fiddling with her cell phone as she waits impatiently for her date. It's a little stretch of urban paradise for young singles, a concrete beach ornamented with eager voluptuaries on the erotic prowl, but behind the elegant, smoked-glass front door of the mosque men and women kneel, bow down, and supplicate themselves to Allah.

"Blessed are You for your Majesty and Bounty and Infinitely flowing generosity, Allah Akbar," sings the sheikha, a thin, pale woman of 56, her head partly obscured by an artfully knotted white *hijab* that overflows her shoulders, from within a circle of worshippers. The proceedings seem simultaneously stiff and informal, and though anyone can wander in off the street, slightly cultish and occult too. If the lights suddenly went out, and a gun shot rang out in the dark—as in a scene from a Graham Greene novel or an early Hitchcock thriller—it wouldn't be entirely surprising.

The mosque's rectangular interior is as sparklingly clean and bright as a SoHo art gallery, with brilliant white walls decorated with large black-and-gold medallions bearing swirls of Koranic script, and a plush red Persian carpet covering the entire floor. In front of the beautifully carved wooden *mihrab* and pulpit is a bouquet of freshly cut yellow roses—an unusually decorative, feminine touch, and an exception to the often dour interior of the typical New York mosque. There are also legless folding chairs so that people can sit on the carpet with the benefit of back support. Most of the men wear white prayer caps, on sale for a couple of dollars just down the street at Sufi Books, while most of the women wear *hijab*s and gowns or loose, comfortable clothes. But at least one younger woman comes in off the street in a tank top, only leisurely covering her head and shoulders with a scarf after she has sat down.

As midnight approaches, the Sufi "ceremony of divine remembrance," known as the *zikr*, begins. The men and women, holding hands, form three concentric circles and start moving from right to left, round and round, executing ritual dance steps and chanting ever more furiously. George, who has come with his wife, hops up and down in a leisurely version of a punk pogoing to the Sex Pistols in 1977. After a while, the three circles come closer and closer, chanting *Hi Hi Hi Hi Hi Hi Hi Hi Hi* over and over again until they have melded into one throbbing, erotically charged whole.

Then the sheikha divides the group into two, each lined up along either wall. "Whoever likes to whirl, come and whirl!" she calls out. First up is José Barrallo, a portly but immensely graceful former Marxist and Muslim convert from Mexico who has donned the ceremonial robes of the Sufi dancer. Gravely, he whirls, alone, for a few minutes in the center of the room, and then everyone joins in. I go outside for some fresh air and strike up a conversation with a man sitting on a bench on the sidewalk. He claims to be a disaffected former member of the Sufi Circle, and starts dishing gossip about the sheikha and the Wahhabis he says have slowly infiltrated the place. Even among the joyously dancing Sufis, it seems, you can't get away from Wahhabis.

The following morning I went to the mosque again for the Friday prayer service. George and José were there, along with a couple of other Sufis, but otherwise, just as Juliet had promised, it was indeed a totally different crowd. The congregation was overwhelmingly Middle Eastern, African and male, and it was so packed inside that the service was held twice, so that two different groups could get in. George, in a crisp white collarless shirt and jeans, looked as dapper as always, and—for now, anyway—as out of place.

EVERYBODY
LOVED HIM
AT THE MARRIOTT

For Charles, Islam had brought meaning, ethics, discipline, purpose and hope to a life that had obviously contained too little of those things before, even if nobody else seemed to have noticed. Over the phone, his 38-year-old brother, Mike, who worked in the computer industry in New York, kept using the word *nice* to describe his kid brother.

"Chuck, for some odd reason, was extremely nice compared to the rest of us," he said musingly, as if he were still scratching his head over it after all these years. "When we were younger, me and my friends used to say, 'How did he become so *nice* when all the rest of us are so aggressive?' One thing I can see when he's with his Muslim friends is he goes out of his way with the kids' fathers to help them with English. He's just always been nice."

Joshua Rhodes, a buddy from Charles' Torrance days, described the L.A. Charles as "a real fun guy. In high school there were cliques, and he had freedom to roam within all the cliques. A little rebellious, not in a political sense, but he had a wild haircut sometimes, jewelry, more of a punk or Goth. He liked hard punk, Sisters of Mercy. Everybody loved him over at the Marriott."

And now everybody loved him at the mosque. Charles *was* nice. He was thoughtful, kind, polite, well-meaning, and intelligent, and had a good sense of humor. Still, I was a little worried about him. Though he was quite articulate, when he talked about the Moroccan—usually referred to vaguely as "my friend" or "my roommate at the time" rather than by his name—he became evasive and spoke stumblingly, as if he were trying to protect not only the Moroccan from scrutiny but also himself.

Several times I asked to meet his friend but was told that he had no interest in meeting me. The same went for Charles' roommate, an Egyptian and, like the Moroccan, also a strict Muslim. Both attended Hunter College—the Moroccan studied physics, the Egyptian biochemistry. According to Charles, they intended to return home as soon as they had their degrees. (The slightly worrying sound of those academic pursuits—physics, biochemistry—brought to mind the Freedom House report on Saudi Wahhabi propaganda, in particular the section informing Muslims that "when they are in the lands of the unbelievers, they must behave as if on a mission behind enemy lines. Either they are there to acquire new knowledge and make money to be later employed in the jihad against the infidels, or they are there to proselytize the infidels until at least some convert to Islam. Any other reason for lingering among the unbelievers is illegitimate.") Nor was I permitted to come to the apartment, which was in a Pakistani-owned building where the FBI not only tapped the phones, he claimed, but occasionally sent an agent over to say hello in person. His roommate's mother was visiting from Egypt, Charles explained, and it would therefore be awkward to have me there. Charles himself wouldn't stay in the apartment if his roommate wasn't present, since being alone with the mother wouldn't be "respectful."

Lately, Charles and the Moroccan had been going to a mosque in Queens housed in what was until recently a liquor store. It was a particularly austere-looking mosque in which a particularly austere form of Islam was preached. Because the people at the mosque followed *Shari'a*, they were considered "extremist," he told me. The sermons there were in Arabic, but someone was usually on hand to translate. The 96th Street mosque, though it was one he would always go to if only because it happened to be near his apartment, had become too mainstream for him. A fortnight after he'd spoken approvingly about al-Yaqoubi, Charles had changed his mind. The Syrian was too open to innovation, to allowing stylistic changes to the religion, and in Islam that is *haram*, forbidden, he said.

The fanaticism, though its expression was muted, was undeniable. He told me how last year he and the Moroccan complained to Abu Namous because there were some photos on display in the 96th Street mosque showing Jordan's Queen Rania on a visit, and there were not supposed to be any pictures in mosques. As Charles remembered it, the Queen might even have been unveiled—another outrage. When they told Abu Namous about it, Namous gently waved aside their objections on the grounds that every religion needed about 5 percent room for deviation, and occasionally you had to bend the rules. According to Charles, the Moroccan's jaw nearly hit the floor when he heard this. Even as he related the story, sitting over a plate of post-Ramadan sushi in an East Village restaurant, Charles' eyes widened in appalled amazement. "Bend the *rules!*" he said, sounding for just a moment like the Californian teenager he must once have been. (For a second, I thought he was about to say, "*Dude!*") "I couldn't *believe* he would say something like that! I was so stunned I didn't even want to shake his hand afterwards!"

Islam is not always political—two weeks after the Friday prayer service, I heard al-Yaqoubi deliver a far milder, actually quite charming sermon on the subject of entertainment, complete with puzzled references to Eminem ("He had a hit song about killing his mother with a shovel. Can you believe it!")—but it's an open question whether it's possible to become a Muslim in America without being influenced by inherently adversarial, anti-democratic Islamic politics championed by Wahhabis. (Sufi Muslims would appear to be the exception, though al-Yaqoubi is strongly influenced by Sufism himself.) "Mosques in Western countries are permeated with Wahhabi 'jihad' rhetoric, encountered the minute one walks in the door," Stephen Schwartz writes in *The Two Faces of Islam.* "Some imams preach jihad; some tolerate it sympathetically; some oppose it privately but are intimidated into permitting it. But it is everywhere. If the imam does not advocate jihad, activists hang out on the premises or on the sidewalks and in the parking lots nearby, spreading the word."

Bruce Randall, the convert who attends Friday prayers at the 96th Street mosque, disputed this. "Politics is not what motivated me to embrace the religion," he said. "I think that political events going on in the world only help our cause, because Americans are not stupid people. They know when they're being fed a line of B.S. It makes people check things out for themselves, see if all the demonization is really true. Does the demonization hurt? Yes, but it cuts both ways, it makes a lot of people question and investigate."

Following his sermon on entertainment, al-Yaqoubi led the assembly in a prayer for the just deceased Palestinian leader, Yasir Arafat. It did make me wonder whether the same would happen if Osama bin Laden passed away—or Saddam Hussein, or al-Zarqawi, the head-chopping leader of the totalitarian, imam-approved Iraqi "resistance." I asked Randall if he was at all bothered by being asked to say a prayer for the late PLO leader. "Arafat's a prominent Muslim," he replied. "Why wouldn't we pray for the death of a prominent Muslim? A couple of weeks ago we did a prayer for the death of a prominent scholar in Medina. We pray for scholars, we pray for leaders."

Randall also disagreed with the idea that al-Yaqoubi's statement about American troops had a political motivation. "I can understand how an outsider would interpret those words in a different way," he allowed, though he himself had only been an "insider" for a month at the time of the sermon. "When I hear the sheikh say that, I'm hearing a leader of my religion saying that God will protect the people who are following his righteous path. To my ears, it's not a political statement, it's a religious one. God will not let Islam be struck down. If there are Muslims being attacked somewhere in the world, He will protect them."

When I pressed him further on how he felt about listening to a Syrian imam implicitly call for the defeat of American troops in the middle of Manhattan, he answered, slightly frostily, that "In America we have this thing called the First Amendment."

And no doubt the sheikh was well aware of it. Listening to him I had the sense that certain

Muslims had studied liberal Western society
the way a military general assesses an enemy
position—probing for strengths and weaknesses,
deciding where and how and at what cost penetration can be achieved.

Even the compliments men like al-Yaqoubi
and Abu-Namous occasionally lavished on
America—how free it was, how generous, how
open to all the peoples of the world, including
Muslims—often seemed calculated and double-
edged, facets of jihad. Could they seriously imagine making Islam dominant in this multicultural
society filled not only with millions who believed
in other gods, but with millions of atheists and
agnostics too? It seemed they could.

And these were the moderates, the "nice"
guys. Al-Yaqoubi was someone with whom I
would have enjoyed a far longer conversation, had
one been possible. Abu-Namous was avuncular
and kind, and always made a point of lightly
touching your hand as he spoke to you. True, his
sense of humor was a little archaic, but at least he
had one and wished to share it. But whether you

were talking with a Kuwaiti imam, a Syrian sheikh or— as I did on the night of the Iraqi vote on the new constitution—with a couple of Muslim friends, the line was more or less identical.

"America is for *everybody*," one of them declared as we sat outside an East Village falafel joint drinking mint tea in the autumn chill. "America belongs to the world." And not only did America have no right to invade a Muslim country—not even Afghanistan after 9/11—it had no right to resist the encroaching Islamization of its own society, either. After all, it wasn't its *own* society—it was everyone's—and men like these were walking encyclopedias of every atrocity the West had ever committed. Genocide against the Native Americans. The enslavement of Africans. The Crusades, the Inquisition, the World Wars, Hiroshima. And the Arabs? Hadn't they ever done any harm in their imperial days, let alone the current era? Not at all, came the answer. When Muslims took over countries, they did so peacefully.

Or, as Charles once informed me, the phrase "Islamic terrorism" is an oxymoron. In Charles' eyes,

Islam could do no wrong because Islam was
wonderful and his own discovery of it a "miracle."
I sometimes thought about his passion for this
religion, to which he was far more dedicated than
the average Muslim, and wondered how it would
all end up. "A lot of Muslims don't know a damn
thing about the political side of Islam," said Peter
Leitner, meaning that they were unaware of the
extent to which the religion had been infiltrated for
political purposes. "Politicization is almost always
part of the package," said the Islamic Supreme
Council of America's Mateen Siddiqui, referring
to hardcore Islamic converts. But if al-Yaqoubi felt
comfortable stating in front of 1,300 people in the
heart of mainstream American Islam that
American troops would be defeated wherever they
went, then what might be said in Arabic in small,
obscure mosques in Brooklyn, Queens and elsewhere with a translation murmured into a pale,
friendly, naive American ear?

But perhaps there was no need to say anything.
When I asked Charles what *he* thought about
al-Yaqoubi's statement, he answered, with a touch

of defiance, that he felt just fine about it. "I *do* wish the American troops would be defeated," he told me, adding, "I'm a Muslim first, and I just live in this country." (If he could find a bumper sticker that read "AGAINST THE TROOPS," he said, he'd put it on his cab.) And were he ever to find himself in the Middle East, let's say, in Iraq, would he fight against American soldiers? "If there was a jihad," he replied evenly, "I don't see how I could not join in."

ENDNOTES

1   Marina Jimenez, *The National Post*, Jan 19, 2002.

2   "Terror in America (26) Muslim American Leaders: A Wave of Conversion to Islam in the U.S. Following September 11," Middle East Media Research Institute, November 16, 2001, available at *http://memri.org/bin/articles.cgi?Page=subjects&Area=middleeast&ID=SP30101.*

3   Press release, "Number of American Mosques Grows by 25%," Council for American-Islamic Relations, April 26, 2001.

4   Jean-Michel Berthoud, "Le Coran plutôt que la Bible," Swissinfo.org, available at www.swissinfo.org/sfr/swissinfo.html?siteSect=111 &sid=5403536.

5   Amy Argetsinger, "Muslim Teen Made Conversion to Fury," *The Washington Post*, Dec. 2, 2004.

6   Saraji Umm Zaid, "Why Every Mosque Should Be Women-Friendly," *Taking Back Islam*, (New York: Rodale, 2002), pp. 109-10.

7   *Latino Muslim Voice*, Jan-March 2005 newsletter,
    available at http://www.latinodawah.org/newslet-
    ter/ jan-mar2k5.html.

8   Jane I. Smith, *Islam in America*,
    (New York: Columbia University Press), p. 161.

9   Ibid., p.171.

10 Alex Alexiev, "London Lessons Lost,"
    Center for Security Policy, available at
    http://www.centerforsecuritypolicy.org.

11 Saudi Publications on Hate Ideology Invade
    American Mosques, Freedom House, 2005,
    p. 57 & p. 83, available at
    http://www.freedomhhouse.org/religion.

12 David Pryce-Jones, "The Islamization of Europe,"
    Commentary, Dec. 31, 2004.

13 Jean Chichizola and Jean-Marc Leclerc, "Bruguière:
    'La menace terroriste est élévee," *Le Figaro*,
    October 5, 2005.

14 "Al Qaeda Builds a Euro Army," *Debka-Net-Weekly*, February 25, 2004.

15 Kate McGeown, "Jack Roche: The naive militant," *BBC News Online*, June 1, 2004.

16 Jean-Pierre Obin, "Les signes et manifestations d'appartenance religieuse dans les établissements scolaires," Ministère de l'éducation nationale, June 2004, available at http://www.proche-orient.info/images/mbd/rapport_obin.pdf.

17 Abdal-Hakim Murad, "The Fall of the Family (Part II)," *Islam for Today*, available at www.islamfortoday.com/murad08.htm.

191

ACKNOWLEDGEMENTS

I would particularly like to thank Tom Christie, who edited the original article, and the *Weekly*'s editor-in-chief, Laurie Ochoa, for first giving me the opportunity to explore this largely uncharted territory.